Samuel Whiton

Glimpses of West Africa

With sketches of missionary labor

Samuel Whiton

Glimpses of West Africa
With sketches of missionary labor

ISBN/EAN: 9783337124625

Printed in Europe, USA, Canada, Australia, Japan

Cover: Foto ©Andreas Hilbeck / pixelio.de

More available books at **www.hansebooks.com**

GLIMPSES

OF

West Africa.

WITH

SKETCHES OF MISSIONARY LABOR.

BY

REV. SAMUEL J. WHITON.

AMERICAN TRACT SOCIETY,

150 NASSAU STREET, NEW YORK.

CONTENTS.

PREFACE.

THE larger portion of the following pages was written during odd moments, snatched from the pressing cares and labors of a missionary life in West Africa. The remainder has been prepared since failing health compelled my return to America.

This little volume does not profess to be an exhaustive or scientific treatise on West Africa, but merely to give a few glimpses of that strange, wild land, and its degraded inhabitants, — such as I have been able to gather during my missionary residence and travels there.

These chapters relate mostly to the country and tribes in the vicinity of the MENDI MISSION, between six and eight degrees north latitude. Other parts of the coast differ, perhaps, in some respects, though the general features are much the same.

If these pages shall arouse in any heart a deeper interest in Africa and the missionary work there, the author will feel that he has not labored in vain.

S. J. W.

WESTFORD, CONN.

GLIMPSES OF WEST AFRICA.

CHAPTER I.

THE COUNTRY.

EARS ago, in a brown school-house, thousands of miles distant among New England hills, I well remember how we used to gaze at the map of Africa, and what a mystery seemed to surround it. Here and there along the coast, rivers and towns were marked down, but the interior was one vast blank. A vail of impenetrable darkness concealed it, and the few remarks that were given only made it appear wilder and more mysterious. Asia and the islands of the sea were looked at in a different light, for much more was known concerning them. Since then, great progress has been made in the exploration of Africa. Liv-

ingstone has penetrated the jungles and kraals
of the south ; Krapf and Burton and Speke
have journeyed far inland from the east; Barth
and Gerard, from the north, have visited and
explored countries before unknown ; and other
venturesome travelers have passed through regions rich and beautiful as Eden, and teeming
with inhabitants.   But there are yet immense
stretches of country where the foot of white
man never trod.   Africa is still a wild, mysterious land.   Its lofty mountains rise in silent
grandeur, seen only by the dusky heathen.   Its
silvery lakes repose in beauty, disturbed by
naught save the light canoe.   Its majestic rivers roll down luxuriant valleys, where no sound
is heard but the wild song or fierce war-cry of
untamed men.   Its crowded towns and villages
are the scenes of many horrid customs and
cruelties.   The tropic sun looks down upon a
region where nature spreads her rarest beauties ; but over all, like a pall of death, rests the
cloud of heathenism.

No country in the world affords a grander
field for missionary enterprise than Africa.   It

stretches through seventy-one degrees of longitude, and seventy-two of latitude. Its population is estimated to be two hundred millions, but very few of whom can be called even nominal Christians. Nearly all are heathens or Mohammedans. It is true that great difficulties lie in the way of christianizing Africa. An enfeebling climate, wild beasts and wilder men, toils, sufferings, privations, disappointments, and death itself, — these the missionary must expect to meet. But God's commands are imperative. "Go ye into ALL the world, and preach the gospel to every creature." He did not say, Go to the pleasantest spot you can find, go where it is very healthy, — ah, no! "The soul that sinneth, it shall die," was as surely spoken of the benighted millions of Africa as of those of more salubrious climes. These millions must not be left to perish in darkness. *Africa must be redeemed*, though thousands shall fall in the holy work. The sweet story of the ˙ cross must be repeated from hill-top to hill-top, and from valley to valley, till her sons and daughters shall sit at Jesus' feet, clothed and

in their right mind. Paul faced perils unnumbered, shrank not from death itself, gloried
in his crosses, and was willing to become all
things to all men that he might save some; and
so should the church of to-day lay its all at the
Saviour's feet, and, asking not why or wherefore, go forward in the simple path of duty.

The very name of WEST AFRICA carries an
indefinable feeling of half-dread to many a
heart. So much has been said of its deadly
climate, and so many have early fallen on the
coast, that some good men have been ready to
advise the abandonment of the field, and the
concentration of forces in a more favored spot.
The country is doubtless unhealthy, and of
many an ardent young missionary it might be
truly written, —

> " He, the young and strong, who cherished
>   Noble longings for the strife,
> By the wayside fell and perished,
>   On the threshold march of life."

But it should be remembered that not one has
fallen in vain. Being dead, they yet speak.
From their lonely graves beneath the palm and

cocoa go forth potent voices, speaking of a life of toil and suffering, and an early death in a foreign land, for what?—for the privilege of telling of Christ to those who sit in darkness and the shadow of death. The eye of Him who notes even a falling sparrow never overlooks the herald of the cross. And besides, the unhealthiness of the coast is often exaggerated. Many are able to live and labor here for years. It is with the hope of awakening in some heart a deeper interest in West Africa and its perishing thousands, that these few sketches of the country and people are written.

Bishop Heber, in that beautiful hymn that has become the rallying cry of missions, sings of the land,—

> " Where Afric's sunny fountains
> Roll down their golden sand."

West Africa is truly a sunny land, and nature has done much to make it lovely to the eye. To the traveler, approaching the coast after tossing for weeks or months on the bois-

terous ocean, it seems almost a paradise. Here
and there the mountains jut boldly down to the
shore, covered with the wealth of tropic vegetation ; and anon there is a level line of coast,
on which the graceful palms stand like sentinels against a background of softly-tinted sky,
while the blue hills rise dimly in the distance.
The quaint villages, with their brown walls and
thatched roofs, repose amid groves of orange
and cocoa, surrounded by little patches of cultivated ground. Now and then green islands
lie like gems in the smooth sea. Gorgeous
flowers, of all the hues of the rainbow, bloom
on the hill-sides and in the valleys. And over
all rests the full, rich light of the tropic sun,
making everything seem yet more beautiful.
No wonder that the new-comer, standing on the
deck of an in-bound vessel, and gazing on all
this loveliness, feels his heart glow with rap-
ture.

West African scenery, as a general rule, looks
best at a distance. When the traveler walks
among the hills and valleys that looked so fairy-
like from the sea, he finds a dense growth of

bushes, and tall, rank grass and weeds, through which it is often difficult to force his way, and which hides the prospect beyond. Poisonous snakes crawl through the jungles. Some of the gayest flowers have no fragrance. At places, the air is laden with miasma. But notwithstanding this, there is much to charm the senses. The idea suggested to the mind is that nature has been prodigal of her gifts, everything is so rich, so gorgeous, so abundant : —

"A world of wonder, where creation seems
 No more the works of Nature, but her dreams;
 Great, wild and beautiful, beyond control,
 She reigns in all the freedom of her soul,
 Where none can check her bounty when she showers
 O'er the gay wilderness her fruits and flowers."

Much of the country bordering on the sea is low and swampy. The banks of the rivers, near their mouths, are lined with the mangroves, which vary in size from a bush to trees a foot and a half in diameter. The roots branch out several feet from the surface of the earth, and, interlacing with each other, form an impenetrable net-work. The mangroves are never found beyond the reach of salt water. Some of the land is so low as to be overflowed during the rains, and other parts are elevated and capable of cultivation through the whole year. Native villages are scattered all over the lowlands, and a few foreign traders have established themselves in the healthier localities. A few miles from the sea, the country is more broken and hilly, and the scenery more varied. There are vast forests of lofty trees, so dense that the missionary can walk through them at noon-day without feeling the heat of the vertical sun. Clear sparkling brooks go rippling along their pebbly beds, furnishing delicious drink for the weary traveler. The towns are larger and better built, and the people more intelligent. A trip among the hills is full of interest and adventure, and gives one an insight into African life that could not be gained by a residence of years on the coast.

West Africa is rich in large rivers, which drain the vast interior regions; but scarcely one has been explored to its source. They are thickly lined with populous towns, and the

scenery is often enchanting. Giant cotton-trees
tower towards the sky, the palm, cocoa and orange are abundant, and flowering vines and
shrubs line the banks. As the missionary
journeys up and down these rivers, telling of
Jesus in town and village, scarcely a sign of civilization meets his eye. The light log canoe
of the native skims over the smooth water, and
sometimes the heavier boat of a trader, laden
with palm-oil or rice, glides slowly along, pro-
pelled by half-naked oarsmen. Amid all the
beauties of the scenery, however, there is always enough of heathenism visible to sadden
the heart.

CHAPTER II.

WEST Africa is a land of everlasting summer. The forests never lose their robes of green. The flowers are forever budding and blooming. No cold winds ever sweep over its hills and valleys. The torrid sun, day by day and year after year, pours down its fierce rays, except when obscured by clouds. The heat is often very intense, the mercury rising above ninety degrees in the coolest part of the house. It seldom falls below seventy-five degrees ; thus making the temperature quite even. There is usually a light breeze, which tempers the heat of the sun. The nights are sometimes so warm, and mosquitoes so abundant, that it is difficult to sleep. It is dangerous for foreigners to expose themselves to a

noon-day sun without some protection from its
rays; but the natives will work all day with
uncovered heads, or sleep out of doors, with the
utmost impunity. The want of cold water is
severely felt by those coming from higher lati-
tudes. Often, when the fever has been burning in my veins, have I felt that I would give
almost anything for a cup of water from the
mossy well of the old New England homestead.
Much of the water on the West African coast
is impure, and has an unpleasant taste, though
there are some clear, sparkling springs

Every one notices the absence of twilight in
Africa. Those beautiful, dreamy hours of more
northern lands are unknown here. When the
sun sets the night shadows gather thickly and
rapidly, and soon there is no sign of day in the
west. But the nights are often extremely
beautiful. The air is soft and mild, and the
moon shines with a fuller, richer light than at
home. The following extracts from my journal
will show, more clearly perhaps than I otherwise can, the beauty of these nights: —

" Last evening as I stood at our wharf, lis-

tening to the sound of distant oars, it seemed
that never before had I seen anything so strange-
ly lovely. Above stretched the heavens, un-
commonly blue and clear, and dotted with
sparkling stars. The tropic moon threw a
flood of magic light on the green islands and
palm-lined shore; the river lay before me blue
and motionless, save as its faint ripples broke
on the white sand at my feet; the heavy thunder of the breakers at Sea Bar, ten miles distant, came to my ear, mingled with wild
snatches of song from a heathen village near
by. How true are those lines by Bishop Heber : —

> ' Every prospect pleases,
> And only man is vile.' "

"Friday morning, at two o'clock, we left
Good Hope for Avery station. It was clear
and still, and the moon shone brightly as
we gave the parting hand to our friends and
glided out on the smooth waters of the Sherbro.
The sky was a deep blue, with white, fleecy
clouds floating through it. No sound broke the
silence save the low voices of our men and the

measured dip of their oars, which sparkled in the moonlight as they rose and fell. The day broke gloriously just after we entered the Bargroo river : — first a faint tinge of light underneath the morning star; then a few crimson streaks creeping up the eastern sky; next a blending of the softest, most wondrous hues stretching well-nigh to the zenith; and finally the majestic king of day riding up the heavens from behind the far-off hills, and reflecting his beams in the calm river along which we were gliding."

Some regard the night air of Africa as almost fatal to foreigners, but I doubt whether the opinion is correct. I have journeyed and slept in open boats on the rivers of this coast at all hours of the night, and was never conscious of any ill effects from the exposure. We always aim, however, to keep at a distance from the miasma-breeding lowlands.

There are but two seasons in West Africa,— the " dries " and the "rains." They each last for about six months. At the beginning and end they are so blended together that it is difficult

3

to fix upon a dividing point. The rainy season begins during the spring months, and the dry season in autumn, though on different parts of the coast the time varies widely; and even in the same place, like northern winters, it is sometimes earlier and sometimes later. The rains commence at the south, and pass up the coast. During their prevalence vegetation thrives luxuriantly. The forests are covered with the densest foliage. Grass, weeds and bushes become rank and tall. Leaves sprout out as if by magic, and grow with astonishing rapidity. Each particle of soil is covered with a mantle of living green, and it requires much labor to keep foot-paths cleared. The swamps and lowlands are flooded with water, but the highlands are so porous that walking is tolerable immediately after the most violent showers.

The quantity of rain which falls is immense, sometimes averaging more than an inch a day for three successive months. It falls, too, with a rapidity exceeding the storms of the United States. The rains, however, are not so constant as many are led to believe. Sometimes they continue for a week with but little cessation, and again there are intervals of bright, beautiful weather, lasting for several days. The pleasant days of the rainy season are more lovely than those of the " dries." The sky is of a darker blue, and the air clearer and cooler ; and nature seems to be more wildly bountiful in her gifts of foliage, flowers, fruits and sunlight, than ever.

Occasional showers occur during the dry season, though sometimes for weeks together not a drop of rain falls. Towards its close the grass becomes dry, and the leaves of some trees grow faded and yellow ; the horizon and distant hills are half obscured by a soft haze, and an air of dreamy voluptuousness reigns around. The constant heat of the vertical sun is very oppressive, and brings on a feeling of languor and weariness. Houses crack, and everything becomes so parched that the first showers are hailed with joy. The dry season is the most favorable for missionary tours through the country, for during the rains the paths are often flooded, and the traveler is liable to a drenching

at any moment. The hottest weather is at the
close of the "dries," when sometimes the at-
mosphere is so oppressive that the slightest
exertion bathes one in perspiration. At the
commencement of the dry season a periodical
wind, called the *harmattan*, prevails on a part
of the coast. It is strongest in the early part
of the day, and frequently subsides in the afternoon, when a sea-breeze springs up. This wind
blows from the north-east, and is regarded as
unhealthy by the older foreign residents on the
coast, who often suffer much from fever during
its prevalence. It is so cool as to be very pleasant to those who have lately come from colder
climes, and does not affect them unfavorably.
The natives complain of cold when it blows
strongly. The harmattan has peculiar drying
properties, and gives a parched, cracking sen-
sation to the skin, which at other times is moist
with perspiration. During its prevalence, a
fine, red dust gathers on leaves, clothes, and
houses; sometimes hardly visible, and at others
plainly seen. The theories accounting for this
are various. One is, that the fine dust origi-

nally comes from the great desert of Sahara, which lies in the direction from which the wind blows. The air is very thick and hazy at this season, and it is impossible to see but a short distance. Ships approaching the coast are subject to much danger on this account.

At the beginning and end of the rainy season West Africa is visited by violent tornadoes. They come from the mountains to the east, and pass seaward. Vessels near the coast are occasionally wrecked by them. They often rise suddenly, and rage with great fury, and are a source of much terror to timid people. The following extract from my journal of a coast voyage will give some idea of the character of these storms on the water: —

" As I went upon deck Tuesday morning, I was rejoiced to find the sails full, and felt that buoyancy of spirits which is always produced by a fresh breeze after a calm. I noticed, however, low down in the northern sky, dark, heavy masses of cloud. The wind continued to freshen, and the white foam-caps grew thicker and thicker on the water. We went to breakfast in

excellent spirits, hoping for a favorable breeze
through the day; but on returning to the deck
we found the dark cloud had rapidly risen, and
betokened a squall. Swiftly and more swiftly
the heavy mass mounted the northern heavens,
until its ragged edges almost reached the zenith. Our captain, usually so much at ease,
now stood on the quarter-deck, anxiously watching the rising storm. He had at first been de-
ceived as to its magnitude, as, unlike most tornadoes, it was unaccompanied by thunder; but
now, as a deep green tinge began to show itself
in the lower cloud, the order was given to take
in sail. The sea grew black as ink, dotted here
and there with spots of snowy foam. As far
out as the eye could reach, a long line of vapor
could be seen, rolling down over the dark waters. Nearer and nearer it came, like a mighty
bank of snow gliding over the inky sea. It
was a moment of suspense. If the tornado
struck us under full sail, it would capsize the
vessel, and we were lost. "Hard up! hard
up!" roared the captain to our helmsman, and
the vessel quickly turned its back to the coming

gale, and flew through the boiling waters. "All hands on deck!" "Take in everything!" —and the stentorian voice rang loud above the roar of wind and waves. For a moment all was confusion. The loud-toned commands for furling the different sails, and the ready response of " Aye, aye, sir!" in swift succession ; the rattling of ropes and creaking of timbers; the heavy tramp of the sailors as they absolutely rushed from one rope to another, would have made the coldest heart beat with excitement. And now the storm was upon us. The wind blew with terrific fury, but the rain fell in such torrents as to prevent the sea from rising to any great hight. As I looked from the cabin window it was a vast, boiling mass of green and white ; but our sails were mostly furled, and we rode safely through it. The gust was soon over, the breeze died away, and again we were on the swells in the heat of a tropic calm. We escaped with the loss of a part of our main-royal and top-gallant sails."

On land, of course, the aspect of the tornadoes is different. Here are two hasty sketches : —

" Wednesday, as I was calling on the heathen people, I heard low mutterings of thunder far to the east among the hills. Looking in that direction, I saw a small arch of black cloud, and underneath a greenish-white tinge. It was rising swiftly toward the zenith, and I hurried homeward. Hardly five minutes had passed before the whole eastern sky was vailed, and a gloom like night rested around us. All was silent, oppressive, breathless. Scarcely a ripple disturbed the glassy smoothness of the river. Nature seemed suddenly paralyzed, waiting for some awful outburst. First came a light puff of air, then another, and another, stronger and yet stronger. Curling waves swept along the inky river, the tree-tops swayed wildly, and the little islands a half-mile away were vailed with storm-clouds. Doors and windows were hastily closed, and the tornado burst upon us in all its fury. The scene was awfully grand. Nature was holding a carnival of wildness. Fierce gusts of wind raged and roared among the trees, stripping them of branches, scattering rubbish in every direction, and shaking the house with their power. The rain fell in sheets, whirling and flying hither and thither, and deluging the earth. Flashes of lightning followed each other in quick succession, and now and then above the roar of the tempest we could hear the loud roll of the thunder. The storm lasted nearly an hour, and then came a calm. The next day marks of the tornado could be seen everywhere. Houses were partially unroofed, and trees prostrated."

"On Sunday afternoon a fearful tornado swept up from the south. The morning had been hot and bright, and the air close and stifling. About three P. M. we heard thunder muttering in the distance, and in a few minutes the hurricane was upon us. It was awfully wild, fully coming up to those descriptions that are sometimes regarded as fabulous. The rain fell in masses; the wind whirled and raged with terrific violence, tearing large branches from trees, unroofing houses, and carrying everything before it; the lurid lightning flashed incessantly, and the thunder roared and crashed and rattled in one continuous peal. A dark-

4

ness like night settled round, and the noise of
the elements was deafening. It lasted an hour,
sometimes partly dying away, and again renew-
ing its violence. The quantity of rain which
fell must have been enormous. The wind tore
off the iron roofing of the mission-house like
paper. In the country villages around, much
damage was done. Many houses were unroofed,
and some torn down, and numerous trees were
prostrated."

The most lovely weather often succeeds these
torrid storms. The sky is a dark, rich blue,
with silvery clouds floating here and there.
The sunlight dances and glimmers on the graceful groves of palm and cocoa. The giant cotton-tree puts on a fresher green, and its smooth
leaves glisten in the light. Gorgeous flowers
bloom on every side, and the breeze is fragrant
with the breath of orange-blossoms. All is
quiet, calm, beautiful, almost fairy-like, — a
perfect contrast to the fierce strife of the preceding day.

Gales of wind are not experienced on this
coast, but during the rainy season the wind

sometimes blows strongly from the south. In the dry season, northerly winds prevail.

West Africa has been called "the white man's grave," on account of the large number of foreigners who have died here. Fever and dysentery are the two great scourges of the climate. All who come must expect to go through a season of acclimation; but many become so habituated to the country as to live here in tolerable health for years. There are those who have resided on the coast for twenty or thirty years, and bid fair to live for as many more. Others are compelled to leave at once or die. So much has been written of the deadly nature of the climate, that many come with a morbid fear, which greatly tends to shorten their lives. Some, if attacked with the dreaded "fever," become so frightened as to give up all hope of life, and of course they die; for the mind exerts a wonderful influence over the body in this disease. A cheerful, hopeful spirit is absolutely indispensable in African fever. Care and prudence will do much towards the preservation of life, and yet those who are the most tremblingly

careful and over-cautious are usually the first
to fall.   The missionary, from the nature of his
work, is obliged to pass through many expo-
sures; and he will find that a firm, childlike
faith in such promises as are contained in the
ninety-first Psalm, together with a quiet prudence, will be far better than over-anxiety and
extraordinary measures.   The young missionary
is often sorely perplexed by the advice of his
friends.   One says, " You must do this, but you
must not do that;" another says, " You must
do that, but not this."   And nearly all unite in
believing that in either case he will be quite
sure to die.   We say, *Expect to live;* make
yourself as familiar with the country as possible; and then use your own common-sense,
with a humble trust in God.

The African fever bears a strong resemblance
to the " fever and ague " of the Western States
of America.   Aching limbs, a general feeling
of lassitude, and a restlessness of mind which
makes it impossible to remain in one position
for any length of time, are certain signs of its
approach.   A chill, more or less violent, usually

succeeds, followed by high fever. As the fever passes off, profuse perspiration sets in, and the sufferer feels easier. The fever is often accompanied with violent pains, and lasts from a few hours to two or three days. A second, third, and fourth attack follow the first in quick succession, unless powerful remedies are applied. Quinine is generally regarded as the best remedy, and sometimes requires to be administered in very large doses. If taken in season it will often prevent the attack.

The missionary must expect to suffer more or less from this fever; and sometimes, when work presses upon him, he will be compelled to leave all, and lie on a bed of sickness. But there will be many hours of joyful labor for his Master, richly repaying him for all his weariness and pains.

CHAPTER III.

THE productions of West Africa are numerous. The soil is usually rich, and if fully developed would yield an almost unlimited amount of produce. No winter retards the growth of vegetation, and there may be a constant succession of crops during the whole year. Perhaps no country in the world is more prolific. But its resources are so undeveloped that years must pass by before the world will really know what West Africa can produce.

The native methods of farming are very simple and imperfect. The wants of the African in his heathen state are so few, and nature goes so far towards supplying them, that he has but little motive for exertion. The same spot of

30

ground is cultivated only a year at a time, and then left to grow up to "bush." Each town or village has its farm, sometimes quite extensive, where the people raise their rice, cassada, sweet potatoes, and other food. The farms are often situated a long distance from the town. The land is first cleared up with hatchets and cutlasses, and afterwards burned over. Almost the only implement used in planting is a small hoe two or three inches in diameter. With this the ground is dug over, and the seed covered. A few rude buildings are usually erected near by, called "farm-houses;" and during the season of planting and harvesting, many of the people remain at the farm for days and weeks, so that the towns are nearly deserted. Others go in the morning and return at night.

Sometimes at sunrise a curious procession may be seen passing towards the farm. A few men go straggling along, much at leisure; naked children with large baskets on their heads, and women, some with infants strapped on their backs, and some bearing heavy burdens, follow; and all have a wild, heathen look.

At night they return, perhaps chanting some
rude melody, and bringing baskets of rice and
sweet potatoes, and hampers of cassada.

Rice may be called the bread of West Africa.
It is raised in larger quantities than any other
article, and is often exchanged by the country
people for cloths and other manufactures of
civilized lands. It is sown at the commencement of the rains, and ripens at the close. A
single farm among the hills often covers forty
or fifty acres. The rice-planting is very laborious, as the seed must all be dug in with the
small native hoe; and after the new rice forms
a constant watch must be kept, or the rice-birds
will devour it. Children frequently do the
watching, and the traveler passing up the rivers
sees them here and there, like statues of ebony,
standing on a rock or stump among the rice.
The harvesting is also laborious. The heads
are clipped from the stalk, and the rice afterwards beaten out on the ground. After this it
requires to be separated from the hull by pound-
ing in a mortar.

Sweet potatoes are abundant, and will ripen

at all seasons of the year. Indian corn flourishes everywhere, but is seldom raised in large
quantities, though from some parts of the
coast it is exported. A small grain called
pota is cultivated, and sometimes eaten in the
place of rice; also the bene-seed, which pro-
duces a kind of oil, and is used by the natives
in their sauce; and the guinea corn, or "koos-
koos." Ground-nuts are produced in large
quantities, and exported by cargoes to foreign
countries. They grow luxuriantly, the tops
resembling rank clover, and the nuts forming
in the ground. They are much used as food.

English and American garden vegetables are
unknown among the natives, but are cultivated
with some success by foreign residents. Efforts
have been made to introduce Irish potatoes, but
those raised have been few and imperfect.

The arrow-root flourishes well, and might be
produced in unlimited quantities. The ginger
of this coast is of a superior quality. Cassada
is largely cultivated in all the native farms,
and is eaten raw, roasted, and boiled. It grows
to be a large bush, and is propagated by plant-

5

ing pieces of the woody stem in the earth. The root is the portion used for food, and it is highly prized by the people.

The coco and the yam are two other esculent roots, largely produced in West Africa. The former is the best substitute for Irish potatoes. The latter is coarse, dry, and insipid. The vine of the yam bears a strong resemblance to pole-beans. Sugar-cane grows well on the coast. It is raised by the natives for eating in small quantities, but the process of sugar-making is unknown to them. In Liberia considerable sugar is manufactured by the colonists for export, and many mills have been established. The indigo plant grows in abundance all over the country, but not much effort has been made to prepare it for exportation. Pepper and coffee can be produced to almost any amount. The latter is now largely cultivated on some parts of the coast. Cotton has long been raised by the natives, and used by them in the manufacture of cloths. The Egyptian and sea-island varieties have lately been introduced, and have flourished to some extent.

The experiments have not been fully tested. The native cotton is of a fine texture, and can be obtained in large amounts.

Many of the productions of West Africa are as yet undeveloped, but vast sources of wealth will doubtless be found in these in the future. There are many fibrous plants, and gums and minerals now almost unknown, which will amply repay the efforts of science and skill to bring them into use. The African fruits are abundant and luscious, but unsatisfying to the foreigner, who longs for his native apple, peach, and pear. The orange is one of the most common and delicious fruits of Africa. It grows almost everywhere, and a bushel can often be purchased for an article worth a few cents. Some trees produce two regular crops a year, and some have a constant succession of flowers and fruit. There is a large, sour orange, unfit for eating, which is used for marmalade. Many of the oranges are superior in flavor to the finest found in American markets. The trees are often large and graceful.

The lime is abundant, and largely used by

the natives with their food. "Lime-drink" is
a cooling and healthful beverage for foreigners.
There are various kinds of plums, sweet and
sour, but they are not generally palatable. A
kind of wild fig is also found upon large trees.
Several varieties of cherries are gathered in the
forests, but they are almost wholly unlike the
cherries of America.

The bread-fruit grows luxuriantly in this
country, though it is not found in a wild state.
The tree is graceful and beautiful, and the fruit
when cooked quite palatable, but it bears but
little resemblance to bread. The bread-nut
exactly resembles the bread-fruit outwardly,
but the rind contains several small nuts, which,
when roasted, are eaten.

The mango is another delicious fruit. The
trees are beautifully shaped, and covered with
the densest foliage, affording a cool shade. The
fruit grows in large clusters, and slightly resembles the peach. The guava is also much
valued. It is of the size of a small apple, and
excellent for eating or for jelly. The paw-paw
is a singular fruit somewhat resembling a musk-

melon. The tree is small, with a tuft of leaves at the top and no branches, and the fruit grows in clusters on the trunk. The sour and sweet sop are indescribable fruits, much liked by some, but seldom by the new-comer. The cashew is another singular production, — half nut and half fruit. The pulpy portion is eaten, and the nut at the end forms the seed.

The pine-apple grows everywhere, and is large and delicious; the plants are sometimes two feet or more in hight. The plantain and banana are found near almost every village, and the site of an old town can often be known by the little orchard of bananas remaining. The plants look very beautiful when growing in large numbers, with their immense leaves glistening in the sunlight, and their large clusters of fruit. The tamarind grows in a wild state, and is also cultivated. The cocoa-nut is plentiful, and the trees at a distance can scarcely be distinguished from the palm. They are sometimes found in large groves, and are a beautiful feature in the landscape. There are many varieties of nuts; — among those most prized by the natives are the kolers. These possess a stimulating property, and are chewed by boatmen to keep themselves awake during the night hours. They are often used as gifts by the people, the present of a koler being considered a pledge of friendship.

Among the trees of Africa, the palm stands first. It gives a pleasing, oriental aspect to the shore, when seen from the sea; and in journeying up the rivers, a palm-grove, standing against a sunlit, tropical sky, forms a picture of exquisite beauty. The trees sometimes rise to the hight of sixty or seventy feet. The leaves make an excellent thatch for buildings, and the fiber is used for lines and fish-nets. The nuts yield two kinds of oil, which form an important part of the exports of the country. Cargo after cargo is shipped every year by the traders, who have established factories along the coast. The natives have devised a singular way of climbing the palm-tree to obtain the nuts. They fasten a hoop around the tree and themselves, against which they lean ; then give a spring upwards, then another, and when they arrive at the top they cut the bunch of nuts from the trunk, and let it fall to the ground. Palm wine is obtained by tapping the tree near the top. It is much prized by the people. A sort of cabbage grows from the trunk at the point where the leaves sprout out. When boiled it affords excellent food.

The bamboo can hardly.be called a tree, yet it is a very important plant. Its leaves closely resemble the palm, and form the chief roofing of houses in West Africa. The camwood is found along the coast in considerable quantities. There are also many varieties of forest trees, affording excellent timber.

The descriptions of farming at the beginning of this chapter relate, of course, to the native modes. On many parts of the coast, where civilization has obtained a footing, farms are cultivated in a far better manner. But the work of introducing improvements goes forward slowly, and agriculture is, in general, in a very backward state.

Of the animals of West Africa, the leopard is one of the most troublesome. It roams through

the bush everywhere, and at night prowls
about towns and villages. Children are frequently killed by it, and grown people sometimes attacked. In the interior, the sheep and
goats belonging to a town are herded within
the walls at night to protect them from the
leopards. The skins of this animal are used for
hangings on the walls of kings' houses, and to
cover native stools.

The elephant is found in many parts of the
hill-country, and is eagerly hunted by the natives for its ivory. These hunts are intensely
exciting, and dangerous. It would be almost
impossible for a white man to participate in
them, so dense is the jungle through which the
huge beast plunges. Tigers are said to abound
in some parts, and lions were formerly found in
the mountains of Sierra Leone. Porcupines
are numerous, and often do much damage in
the farms and among the fowls.

Monkeys are common all along the coast;
and the traveler, passing up and down the rivers, hears them chattering in the forests, and
sees them leap from branch to branch. They

are often caught, tamed, and carried to foreign countries. The chimpanzee, which strongly resembles a human being, is also found in the forests; and the ourang-outang is sometimes seen.

There are but few cattle on the immediate coast, but they abound towards the interior. Sheep and goats are very numerous, also fowls. The African sheep closely resembles the American, except that it has no wool, and is covered with fine, smooth hair. Several kinds of deer, and many other animals, larger and smaller, are found on the coast.

The birds of West Africa have often a most gorgeous plumage, but their songs are not so sweet as those of more temperate regions. Among them are the rice-bird, crane, pelican, crow, hawk, vulture, eagle, and pigeon. Many varieties of fish are found in the waters. Sharks are so numerous that bathing and swimming are dangerous, and not unfrequently the natives are killed by them. Alligators are often seen gliding along near the surface of the water, or sunning themselves on the banks. The

6

hippopotamus, or river-cow, is a native of the country; and its hoarse bellowings are heard during the night hours by the traveler as he lies in his little boat.

The insects and reptiles of West Africa are a terror to many foreigners. They are very numerous, often troublesome, and sometimes dangerous. Africa may well be called the land of ants. These little insects are of all shapes and colors. They go everywhere. They enter our houses, and glide over the table-cloth as we sit at dinner. They pass up and down the walls, cross the mat-covered floors in continual processions day and night, and crawl over our portfolios as we write. Our paths are lined with them, whenever we walk out of doors; and the rock or log on which we seat ourselves to rest is sure to have an abundant supply.

The drivers are a curious species of African ants. They are medium sized, but very ferocious. They travel in a long, close line, about half an inch wide. These processions often cross and re-cross a path many times, and as they move swiftly forward over the same spot

hour after hour, their numbers must be immense. If anything disturbs their line of march,
they rush out in every direction with amazing
swiftness to attack the intruder. Whatever
comes in their way is eagerly devoured. Bugs,
worms, serpents, and even goats and sheep if
taken in an unsuspecting moment, are instant-
ly covered with myriad swarms, and struggle
in vain to escape. Even the huge elephant and
boa-constrictor are said to have sometimes fallen a prey to the innumerable legions of these
tiny animals. An experienced eye is almost
certain to detect the long black line of drivers
winding across the path; but if in a thought-
less moment the traveler's foot is placed upon
it, a scene at once painful and ludicrous follows. In an instant his body is covered from
head to foot, and a hundred sharp fangs pierce
his flesh, causing involuntary screams, jumps,
and most undignified antics, that draw roars of
laughter from the most sympathizing looker-on.
But all is in vain. No relief can be found by
the victim, whose excited imagination fancies a
hundred bites for one, till he retires by himself,

and picks off the clinging drivers one by one. Sometimes they enter houses, and effect a good purpose by clearing them of roaches, bugs, and smaller ants.

The bug-a-bug is another wonderful and troublesome ant found in West Africa. It does much damage to the wood-work of houses, not unfrequently destroying it altogether. The native houses last but a few years on account of the depredations of these ants, and great care has to be exercised in the mission-houses to keep them out. They form a little arch of mud along the walls and floors, underneath which they come and go, preying upon the wood. Sometimes they enter a post from the earth, and devour all the inner portion, while the outside seems as solid as ever, till suddenly it falls. Like the drivers, they are small, but their name is legion.

The bug-a-bugs show a wonderful industry in building their houses, which are called " bug-a-bug hills." These hills are numerous almost everywhere; sometimes an acre of land will contain a score of them. They vary much in size and shape. Some are fourteen feet high, twenty or thirty in circumference at the base, and have many little spires and pinnacles. They are built of a brown clay, quite hard, and often present a really beautiful appearance. The building of these solid hills by such tiny insects is a wonder next to the formation of coral islands. Each hill has its "queen," — a bug-like animal, two or three inches in length. At certain seasons of the year winged bug-a-bugs issue in immense numbers from small holes in the ground, but after a few hours' exposure to the air the wings fall off. At this time they are gathered by the natives in large quantities, parched, and eaten as food. They are regarded as very delicious.

The serpents of this country are of all sizes, from the minutest to the huge boa-constrictor. Some are harmless, and the bite of others is deadly. They abound in all the fields and forests, yet very seldom is any one injured by them. The natives go everywhere barefooted, but are rarely bitten, and I never heard of a case that resulted fatally. Scorpions are often

found in houses, and among books and clothing; centipedes are also numerous. But these
poisonous creatures give the foreign resident
far less trouble than the swarms of mosquitoes
which gather round at nightfall. Along the
rivers and lowlands they are sometimes almost
unendurable, and all efforts to exclude them
prove fruitless. There are many other insects
and reptiles, large and small, which would afford
the student of nature a wide field of exploration.

The modes of traveling in this country are
few and simple. They may almost be reduced
to two, boating and walking, though palanquins,
sedan-chairs and hammocks are used in many
places by foreigners, and in three or four of the
most civilized towns there are a few horses.
The swinging palanquin, borne by two carriers,
is an easy mode of journeying in the mountain
districts; but it is not usually available. A
sort of hammock, suspended from two poles,
which are borne on the shoulders of four natives, is often used; but there are many paths

so narrow and overhung with bushes that walking is the only method of passing over them.

The term *road* in Africa means simply a foot-path; there is nothing in this country similar to the wide carriage-roads of America and England. Even in the partly civilized towns, the streets consist of a wide walk in the center, somewhat resembling an American sidewalk except that it is unpaved, and on either hand is a grass-covered space. The native roads, which lead from town to town, are the narrowest and most crooked of foot-paths. They are often completely overhung and crowded with bushes, which sweep the traveler on either side as he passes. They wind round and round, making the sharpest of angles, and as new paths occasionally branch out just when one has lost all idea of the points of compass, a guide is absolutely necessary.

The missionary sometimes journeys over these paths, in order to visit towns which are not accessible by boats. Such trips are wearying, but at first full of interest and novelty. Having made your baggage as light as possible, remem-

bering to supply yourself with a little food, you
secure six or eight men and set forward. The
guide leads the way, and the rest follow in single file. One man carries a small basket, or
" bly," as the African calls it, containing your
provisions, on his head ; another balances your
valise in the same manner ; another carries
your shawl and pillow ; a fourth has a glass
lantern in his hand ; and the others are laden
with various small articles. You spread your
umbrella to keep off the fierce rays of a torrid
sun, but soon you enter the " bush," and find-
ing it a burden, you close and hand it to one of
the men. You feel in fine spirits, and press
forward rapidly. The forest is very dense, and
the air seems refreshing. Now and then you
catch sight of your shawl and pillow disappear-
ing round some sharp angle, or hear the shrill
cry of the guide in advance, and the answering
echo from the rear. Sometimes you walk along
a soft leaf-covered path, and anon stumble over
tangled roots and loose stones. One moment
you almost lose trace of the path, and are compelled to force your way through what seems

an impenetrable jungle ; the next you clamber up the branches of a huge tree which has fallen across the way, and walk along the trunk for thirty or forty feet. Shady as is the road, the perspiration rolls down your face ; and when you reach a mountain stream, rippling over its rocky bed, you are glad to stop and drink from the tin cup that you did not forget to put in the "bly." Presently you cross a deep gorge on a log, and climb a steep, rocky hill. By and by you come to a swamp, where the path is wet and miry. One of your sturdiest men comes to the rescue, takes you on his back, and trotting slowly through the mud, deposits you dry-shod on the opposite shore. Thus you journey hour after hour, sometimes passing through an open field where the sun's rays are intensely hot. At length you approach rice and cassada patches, and meet natives more frequently, — sure signs that a town is near. You send a small present to the king, and he provides a house for you to rest in, after which, perhaps, you preach to the people, who gather to hear, of Christ and him crucified.

7

A white man, in these trips, is an object of the greatest curiosity to the people. The few natives whom he meets by the way stare eagerly, and sometimes at first sight spring back in terror. Crowds gather round him as he enters a town, and frequently almost the entire population follows him as he leaves. These escorts are often attended with the most extravagant noises and shouts, running and jumping. I hardly ever walked in an interior town without a curious group following my steps, and watching every motion. If I seated myself for a moment in a " barre," they would pause, chatter away in their native tongue, and laugh, doubtless busy with their comments on the queer dress and manners of the white man. The children, especially, are terrified at a white face. They will gather in groups at a safe distance, and peer round some corner with gaping mouths and wide-open eyes; but the slightest demonstration of approach, or even a steady gaze, is enough to send them away screaming with fright. I have often been amused, while resting in these towns, to see the parents bring their " piccaninnies" towards me ; the moment they caught my eye the invariable scream burst forth, which was the signal for a general shout of· laughter from the gathered crowd.

The natives travel with great ease over these rough paths, often walking twenty-five miles a day for many days in succession. Though always barefooted, their feet seldom become travel-worn. They do not usually carry heavy burdens, but if necessary they show a surprising power of endurance. I once had a sheep presented me by the king of a large walled town in the interior, and, as it could not be made to walk, the king's son carried it on his back a distance of thirty miles over a rough path in a single day! The kings, like their subjects, must walk, for the natives have no mode of riding except in canoes.

The most common way of traveling near the coast is in boats and canoes. In many places, one can hardly visit the nearest villages without a short trip on the water. The numerous rivers and winding creeks greatly facilitate this mode of journeying. The missionary often goes hundreds of miles in his open boat, protected from sun and storm only by an awning. Sometimes the boat is his home for many days together, and he must learn to make himself comfortable in a small space. Boat traveling has its pleasures, and, particularly in the rainy season, its manifold discomforts. The experienced resident on the coast becomes so accustomed to cramped quarters, occasional drenchings, and eating and sleeping under difficulties, that he scarcely minds them ; but the new-comer finds that the reality of the thing rather outbalances the romance.

You arrive on the coast, perhaps, at the hight of " the rains," and find a journey of one or two hundred miles before you in an open boat. The romance of adventure is not yet dissipated, and you are rather pleased with the prospect. You find yourself in a small cabin, some six feet by four, formed by an awning, with side and end curtains. Several mattresses, blankets, and pillows, somewhat the worse for dampness and mildew, are placed on the seats ; and the space which you do not occupy is piled with trunks, valises, boxes, and baskets. Soon it begins to rain ; and the awning, that was supposed to be water-proof, is found sadly wanting in that respect. You move this way and that, and draw yourself into the smallest possible dimensions; but the little streams come thicker and faster, until yourself and baggage are thoroughly dampened, not to say wet. The ocean grows rough, and the boat begins to toss about like a leaf. The waves break over the bow, and you hear them roar on the rocky beach. Your baggage tumbles about, and the basket containing the crockery and provisions comes down with a crash. Meantime, the rain continues to fall in torrents ; and, half sea-sick, and more than half wet, you feel decidedly uncomfortable, and think that it is pleasanter to read about such things than to pass through them.

By and by it becomes smoother, and you pre pare for dinner. Your boatmen cook some rice and meat, and you draw forth a little bread, butter, and jelly from the canteen ; and, without a table, the boat rocking, and the rain still falling, you eat as best you may. Night comes, dark and wet, and, wrapping yourself in a shawl, you lie down to sleep. Thus you journey, perhaps, for several days, with occasional cessation of rain, and bursts of sunshine.

During the dry season, these boat-trips are far pleasanter. You sit hour after hour on the cushioned seat, gazing on the soft, hazy shore, with its palm-groves and queer-looking towns; or you lie at full length, in a dreamy half-sleep, listening to the dip of the oars and the chants of the men. If you have not forgotten a book or pamphlet, you may spend many a delightful hour in reading. At night, when the stars come out, and the tropical moon floods sea and shore with its full, soft light, you enjoy such a scene of magic beauty as could be found nowhere else.

The preparations for a long journey in a boat require much care, and some experience. Everything must be seen to by your own eye, or the men will be almost certain to neglect it. You have even to watch the boatmen, or they will contrive to be absent at the precise moment you wish to start. Then you must see that they are supplied with rice, water, and salt, and that the boat is properly rigged. Next, you array yourself in your oldest clothes; and, having taken a goodly supply of blankets, pillows, and shawls, not forgetting the canteen of provisions and the water-jugs, you are ready to start, which you do after several "palavers" and unnecessary delays among the men. If your course is up some river, perhaps you stop at a native town to spend the night. The king provides you a house; and, spreading your shawl on a mat on the mud floor, you sleep very comfortably, considering the heathen songs and shouts, that continue till a late hour. In the morning, when you wake, you find the glassless window crowded with black faces, all eager to see the white man or woman. You are anxious to start forward early, but your boatmen have all mysteriously disappeared. You feel a little like scolding, but conclude to make the best of it. After a delay of an hour or two, and sundry tiresome walks, you succeed in getting your men together, and proceed on the journey.

Canoes are universally used by the natives for journeying by water, and are often employed for carrying produce. Some of them are very large, and, with an awning at the stern, afford comfortable quarters for any one. Most of the native canoes are hollowed out of a single log, and vary in size according to the tree from which they are cut. Some are only ten feet in length, by one in width, and others are thirty or forty feet long, and three or four wide. The natives, especially a tribe called Kroomen, manage these frail canoes with great skill. They venture far out at sea, even when the water is rough. Almost the first sight that greets the passenger on an inward-bound vessel is a fleet of these trough like conveyances putting off from the shore. At first they seem mere specks, rising on the crest of a wave, and sinking from sight behind the next. As they approach, the half-naked occupants strain every nerve at the paddles, in an effort to outstrip their neighbors; and the race often becomes exciting. If an overturn happens it matters little, for the Kroomen are as much at home in the water as on land, and will swim about, and right their canoes with ease.

In traveling up the rivers, log canoes are seen loaded with produce and passengers; but accidents rarely happen. By night, a " tom-tom," a sort of drum, is generally beaten, which, blending with the chant of the men, makes a mournful music, as it sounds out on the night air. These canoes present a pretty appearance as they glide swiftly to and fro over the waters.

CHAPTER IV.

TOWNS — HOUSES — MANUFACTURES.

WELL remember how curiously I gazed at the towns of the African coast, when I first saw them from the deck of an English steamer. They are in perfect contrast to the neat, white villages of America, yet they are not altogether destitute of a sort of beauty of their own. Seen from the sea, they harmonize well with the tropical landscape. The small, round houses, with their roofs of thatch, clustered amid groves of orange or palm, and surrounded with a wealth of foliage, charm the eye of the ocean-tossed wanderer as he approaches the green shores. Sometimes the houses are scattered along a hill-side, half vailed with a soft haze; and again they are crowded together in some small opening in the bush.

A nearer view detracts somewhat from the picturesque aspect of these towns; yet even then the smooth, mud walls, and neat pointed roofs, look really pretty. Many of them on the immediate coast, especially in the vicinity of mission stations, show some marks of civilization. The houses are not crowded so close to each other, and often there is space for a little garden-patch, and a cluster of bananas and fruit trees. Sometimes there is a faint attempt at regularity in the streets; but more commonly the houses are scattered about promiscuously, while narrow foot-paths wind among them.

Many of the native towns are walled, or barricaded, to protect them from the attacks of neighboring tribes. Some of these defenses are quite ingeniously constructed, and, though they would offer but little resistance to American weapons of war, they prove formidable here. In some cases, the outer barricade consists simply of large round sticks, ten or twelve feet long, set in the earth close to each other, and firmly bound together. Inside of this is a space some five feet wide, which in case of an attack

is occupied by the soldiers, who thrust their
muskets between the sticks and fire upon the
enemy. The inner wall is solid, being thickly
coated with mud on either side. The infirm
and the children take refuge within, where, unless the place is captured, they are safe. Other
towns have externally a solid wall, inside of
which is a space of perhaps fifteen feet, filled
with sharp sticks pointing in every direction, so
that if an enemy scales the wall and falls, he
will be impaled and killed. Still further in is
a second barricade of sticks. Not unfrequently
a deep ditch surrounds the outer wall. There
are usually several watch-towers, rising above
the highest barricade, in which sentinels are
stationed with muskets to look out for an approaching foe, and alarm the people in case of
danger. The entrances to the town are closed
by solid double doors of wood, which at night
are securely barred. The stranger in entering
must pass through the outer gateway, then
along a narrow passage, often so low that he is
obliged to stoop, and finally through a second
gateway. Several " war-men," armed with cut-

lasses and guns, are generally seen about the
gates, even during the day.

The interior of a walled town is a novel sight.
There is no sign of streets, but the houses are
huddled so close together that their thatched
roofs often touch each other. The ground not
occupied by buildings is smooth and hard, and
scarcely a spire of grass or a weed can be seen.
It is swept each morning by the people, and the
litter of the previous day removed, so that a
neat appearance is presented. A stranger will
be very likely to lose his way as he wanders
among the houses, coming now into a small,
open court, then winding through narrow passages between two mud walls. Here he sees a
kitchen, in which the women are cooking rice
and fish, or tending their naked " piccaninnies," and there another, its exact counterpart.
Women are coming and going, bearing on their
heads bundles of sticks and blies of fruit. Men
are lounging about in the sun, or lying in their
swinging hammocks. Some of the people are
weaving mats and baskets ; others are spinning
yarn from the native cotton.

A large town has usually several unwalled villages under its protection, whose inhabitants, if war comes, flee to it for safety. The size of towns, of course, varies widely. Very few have more than fifteen hundred or two thousand people, and many do not approach these numbers. Villages are often found with only half a dozen houses. Their site is commonly marked by one or two giant cotton-trees, which afford a cooling shade.

The majority of African houses are built in a circular form, and are very small,— only twelve or fifteen feet in diameter. The dwellings of the chiefs, however, and of some of the leading men, are oblong, and much larger. They have a sort of mud-plastered piazza on one side, where visitors are invited to sit, and where the chief spends much of his time, stretched at full length in a hammock. The construction is very simple. A spot is first selected, and cleared of underbrush. A light frame is then put up, consisting of sticks set in the ground close to each other, with slender poles for rafters. The sticks are fastened together by tying them with a kind of vine which is used for rope. The walls are next inwoven with small sticks, and afterwards thickly coated on both sides with mud. This soon hardens, and forms a smooth surface, sometimes brown, and sometimes tinted with yellow. The pointed roof is neatly covered with palm or bamboo thatch, and the floor made of a kind of mud which soon becomes smooth and solid. A rude partition generally divides the house into two rooms. A low aperture is left for the doorway, and perhaps there is one small opening to admit the light. The interior is quite dark, and the people spend most of their time in the open air. Fires, if required, are built in the center of the room, the smoke being left to find its way out as it can. The ends of several long sticks are placed together, and as they burn off, the brands are pushed up, and the fire thus kept burning through the whole night. The smoke is trying to the eyes of a traveler, but it serves to keep off the swarms of mosquitoes.

In the better class of houses, the window apertures are closed at night by wooden shutters,

and a frame-work covered with matting placed
at the doorway. The walls are hung with prettily figured mats and leopard skins. Sometimes the outside of the house is adorned with
a few rude pictures in red and black, and a little attempt at embossing in the mud-work.

Nearly every town has its "kitchens," which
are built much like the houses, except that
they are open on one or two sides. Here the
women do much of their cooking, and a group
of idlers lounge about, chatting or sleeping. A
tub or large bowl of water stands in one part
of the kitchen, with a gourd-shell "calabash"
for a drinking-vessel; and a pot of rice is boiling over a fire in another part.

The public building of the town is called a
"barre," and answers nearly the same purpose
as a court-house. It has a mud floor, thatched
roof, and a few rude seats. Some barres are
open on one side, some on all four; others
are circular in form. Those of the leading
kings are constructed with great care, and look
very prettily. Here the prince, as occasion requires, sits in state and listens to the "palavers"

or disagreements of his people, and decides them. The missionary, too, often avails himself of the barre, where more or less people are usually congregated, to repeat the story of the cross.

It has been said that an African village, seen in the distance, bears a strong resemblance to a collection of weather-beaten hay-stacks; and perhaps this homely comparison will give a better idea of its general appearance than any other. The circular houses, with their pointed roofs of thatch crowned with top-knots, certainly suggest such an idea to a new-comer. In passing walled towns, you see nothing but the high barricade, and a mass of thatched roofs seeming to touch each other everywhere.

The sites of the African towns are constantly changing. Where there is now a large, flourishing town, in a few years there may be nothing but a mass of ruins, rapidly growing up to bush. The construction of houses is so light, and the depredations of insects so great, that they last but a short time; besides, the habits of the people are migratory. The numberless

9

wars of the country, too, destroy many towns, and there seems to be a feeling prevalent which prevents a king from building a new town on the site of one thus destroyed.

The houses of foreign residents on the coast, and of the wealthier class of civilized natives, are commonly constructed of wood or stone, and are two stories high. The lower is used for a store-room, and the family live in the upper part, which is cooler and far more healthy, especially during the rains, when everything near the ground is moldy and wet. An airy piazza runs across one or two sides of the house, affording an admirable resting-place when one is hot and tired. These residences are often richly furnished, and present a striking contrast to the mud huts that surround them. Rich hangings, sofas and chairs, and costly ornaments, adorn the rooms, and one almost forgets for the moment that he is in a heathen land. The mission-houses are plain, but comfortable, though the pioneer of a station must suffer many privations before he can be provided with such a home as his health requires.

The native huts are universally known as "country houses."

The native manufactures of West Africa are few and simple. The heathen, accustomed to a wild, savage life, and living in a hot climate, have but few wants which bounteous nature does not supply, and there is but little incentive to industrious effort. They show much native skill, however, in the articles which they manufacture. Among the most important of these are the "country cloths," made from cotton that grows on the coast. Considering the rude implements for preparing it, this cloth is of a superior quality. The spinning apparatus consists of a short, spindle-shaped piece of wood, having a small weight at the end, through which the point projects. The heavy end is placed on a smooth, solid surface, and the cotton attached to the spindle, which is set in motion by the hand. The spindle is upright when in motion, and falls when it stops, so that an unpracticed workman would make poor progress; but the native women are very expert in managing it. The whole affair is scarcely more than eight inches in length. It might be supposed that the thread thus spun would be poor and uneven, but on the contrary it is quite smooth.

When a sufficient quantity of this thread has been prepared, it is stretched from stick to stick, until a warp of appropriate width, and many yards in length, is formed. This is placed in a rude loom, and inwoven with similar thread. The cloth as woven is only six inches wide, but the strips are afterwards sewed together. The loom, in principle, resembles the old-fashioned hand-loom; but it has no frame, and is so small that it may be rolled up and carried by a little child with ease.

Some " country cloths " are white, some striped and checked, and others have beautifully ornamented and fringed borders. The women show much ingenuity in mingling different colors in warp and filling. These cloths are made in large quantities towards the interior, from whence they are brought to the coast, and sold to traders. They form a large part of the clothing of the people. When fine · and soft, they make handsome table-cloths.

The country blacksmith is another important manufacturer. In some places iron ore is found in abundance ; and when so, it is gathered, placed in a clay pot, and melted. The bellows for fanning the flame is a curious contrivance. It consists of a block of wood with two perpendicular openings, which communicate with a sort of horizontal pipe. A piece of goat-skin is fastened over these cavities. A small hole is left at the top, by which the air enters. The operator puts his hand over the hole, and presses down the skin, thus forcing the air through the pipe upon the flame. As he lifts his hand the air again enters the cavity ; and so, alternately rising and falling, this simple contrivance effects the same purpose as a more pretentious bellows. The forge is a rude fragment of iron, or a stone. Some blacksmiths are quite skillful in the manufacture of hatchets, cutlasses, spears, hoes, and other implements. The native iron is said to be of a superior quality, and knives are sometimes made from it with so keen an edge as to be used for shaving the hair.

Another common article of manufacture is the " country mats." They are made from the bamboo, which is cut when quite small, peeled, dried, and afterwards woven. Some of these mats are quite large, and make an excellent covering for floors in a hot climate. They are woven in different colors and patterns, many of which are really beautiful. The people use them for a variety of purposes, such as tables, seats, and beds. If a stranger visits them, a mat is spread on the mud floor, and a dish of rice and fish set upon it for him to eat. If a " palaver " is held, or a missionary preaches, they sit on their mats to listen. If they wish to sleep, they wrap a country cloth about them, and stretch themselves on a mat.

A variety of " blies," or baskets, are also made from the bamboo. Some are large, and will hold two or three bushels, but more generally they are of a convenient size for carrying on the head. Some are very small, and fancifully woven in different colors. Beautiful table-mats are manufactured from the same substance, also the common country hammock.

A light, graceful stool, of singular construction, and usually covered with matting or leopard skin, is made by the natives. Of the log canoes dug from the trunks of trees, I have before spoken. The process is a very laborious one, but it is performed with much skill.

Towards the close of the dry season, when the swamps are nearly drained of water, large quantities of salt are manufactured on the marshy portions of the coast. I can not better describe the process than by transcribing from my journal the record of a visit to one of these manufactories : —

" Leaving the barre, where I had been engaged in teaching a group of heathen, I set out on a visit to the native salt-works. Accompanied by the chief's son, I walked along the winding paths past clusters of mud-walled, palm-thatched houses, and groups of half-naked people. The tropic sun was still high in the heavens, but an umbrella tempered his fierce rays. As we left the town, our path lay through a dense bush.

" A short walk brought us to the first salt-

pond, — a large, level space, at present destitute of water. This space is overflowed by the
sea at flood tide, and at the ebb the water retires, leaving the ground strongly impregnated
with salt. Crystals of the pure mineral were
glistening in the sunshine as we passed along.
A woman, with a strip of cloth about her waist,
was busily engaged in scraping up the surface-
earth into small heaps, which are afterwards
carried in baskets to the manufactory.

"Just beyond the pond we came upon the salt-
works. Here were long rows of strainers, used
for separating the salt from the dirt. They are
funnel-shaped, some three feet in diameter at
the top and tapering rapidly to a point, composed
of a frame-work of sticks, covered with palm
leaves, and plastered on the inside with mud.
These strainers are suspended over long wooden
troughs, and filled with salt earth scraped from
the pond. Water is then poured on, which
drains slowly through, dissolving and carrying
with it the salt.

"Near by stood the boiling-house, — a long,
low frame-work of poles, covered with palm

thatch, and having mats hung before the door-ways to keep out the wind. Within was a row of large, shallow pans, supported by a sort of white bricks of native manufacture. Hot fires were glowing underneath, rapidly evaporating the water, and leaving pure, beautiful salt. As I stepped into the boiling-house for a moment, the intense heat made me gasp for breath, and I could scarcely understand how those poor people could endure it day after day.

"Much of the salt thus manufactured is sold to the interior tribes for country cloths, rice, and palm-oil. Nearly all the work is done by women and children. The wives of the old chief of Bonthe were toiling in the manufactory which we visited. Of course the surroundings were strange and heathenish, but after all there was much native skill shown in the arrangements."

The ingenuity of the people is shown in the manufacture of a variety of little articles. On some parts of the coast beautiful ear and finger rings are made from native gold. Finger rings are also carved from the palm nut, and large

10

rings for the wrist are made from the hoof of
the elephant. The " gree-grees," " medicines,"
and charms, so universally worn, are made by
particular individuals, upon whom the common
people look with a sort of fear. It is said that
a rude kind of musket is manufactured by the
tribes towards the interior. The children who
have been gathered from heathen homes into
mission schools show a remarkable talent for
imitation, and are able, with a little practice,
to construct *fac-similes* of almost any article
which they see. The faculty of originality does
not seem to be so fully developed, though it is
not entirely wanting. African manufactures
are few and simple, but not to be despised.

CHAPTER V.

THE PEOPLE — DRESS — LANGUAGE — FOOD.

ENTURIES of heathenism have left sad marks on the people of West Africa. This is a trite saying, but it contains more truth than most readers would imagine. The churches at home are accustomed to think of heathen countries as regions of darkness, but they do not fully understand the depth of this darkness. In order to have a true idea of the blight and mildew that rests on everything; to see the terrible dwarfing and crushing power of superstition and ignorance; to fathom the fearful depths to which human beings, unblessed by the gospel of Christ, can descend, — one must himself stand on heathen shores. He must see the people in their homes. He must live among them. He must see with his own eyes, day

after day, the disgusting sights that abound.
He must witness their superstitious ceremonies.
He must learn from personal experience their
deceit and dishonesty. He must strive to make
known the gospel to those who have no spiritual
ideas. And if, in doing this, he does not gain
a new and clearer insight into heathen degradation, it will be strange indeed.

No pen, however gifted, can sketch a perfectly
life-like picture of the people of this country.
There are many little things which baffle descrip-
tion; things that must be seen to be understood.
There can be no comparison with home scenes,
for everything here is in perfect contrast with
them; almost as widely different as if it were
of another world. And beside, though the missionary mingles with the natives daily, and sees
their superstitious customs, yet even he finds it
difficult to ascertain the mental ideas, the heart-
beliefs, that give rise to these practices. It is
easy to glance at the outside surface, but next
to impossible to probe the dark mind of a be-
wildered heathen, who himself, perhaps, has no
clear understanding of the customs that he

blindly follows. Yet the pen is not powerless; and plain, homely sketches of the people and their habits will help to give a glimpse of the condition of West Africa.

The stranger, visiting this country, is struck with the endless variety of costumes, as well as by the lack of all costume. Probably there is no other land in the world where dress differs so widely, or is worn in more ludicrous ways. There are certain styles peculiar to the country, but they are by no means universally followed. Fashion allows every one to dress just as he pleases. Everything which can by any possibility be construed as clothing, is made to answer the purpose, and is worn just as fancy dictates.

Only a little covering is required in so warm a climate, and but little is worn. A single garment often comprises the whole stock. The native country cloth forms the chief portion of it. This varies in size, but is ordinarily about two and a half yards long, by one and a half wide. The men wrap it gracefully around the body, one end falling over the left arm, which keeps it in place, while the right shoulder and arm are bare. When worn in this way it reaches nearly to the ankles, and makes a decent covering. Sometimes the men wear nothing but a narrow strip of cloth about the loins. A sort of shirt, or flowing robe, fashioned from country cloths, is quite common. When the pattern of the cloth is pretty, and, as is frequently the case, it is ornamented in the rude native style, it forms a pleasing though grotesque costume. The Mohammedans, or " murray-men," usually wear a long flowing robe, somewhat ornamented.

The dress of the native women consists merely of a country cloth tied around the waist, and reaching nearly to the feet. The whole upper part of the body is left naked. On the coast, where foreign goods can be obtained, a piece of calico or blue baft is sometimes substituted for native cloth. Among some tribes, girls who are not married wear nothing but two or three strings of beads, or a narrow strip of cloth. Children of both sexes are destitute of any clothing.

African women have their own ideas of beauty, and, like their civilized sisters, some of them spend a good deal of time at the toilet. In walking through a village, one often sees them engaged in painting their faces. They use a white, chalky substance, reduced to the thickness of cream. Some cover their faces with a smooth, even coat, and others draw fanciful figures on the jet-black skin. I have often seen mothers ornamenting their children in this way. They first wash them from head to foot, and then cover their skin with the cosmetic. The children are highly delighted with the operation, but present a queer appearance when it is finished, with their black, woolly hair, rolling white eyes, and shining teeth. A mother who is particularly fond of her child seeks to load it with ornaments. Little bands, called " medicines," are tied around its ankles and wrists ; gree-grees, and strings of shells, bits of money, and little bells,—everything, in short, bright or gay, that the mother's ingenuity can pick up, are hung around its neck and body. Often have I seen a heathen mother's face light up with a smile of pride as she watched her painted little

one go toddling along with its load of " medicines," jingling bells, and rattling shells.

The modes of wearing the hair vary widely.
Sometimes it is left in its natural state, but
commonly the women spend much time in ar-
ranging it. It is worn in braids, and in long
curls, done in a variety of fanciful styles, pointing in every direction. The heads of the children are frequently shaved. Sometimes the
top of a man's head is bare, while a ring of hair
is left just above the neck; others have a tuft
of hair on the crown, and the rest closely shaved.
Turbans, fashioned from gay-colored handkerchiefs, are very popular among the women,
whenever they can be obtained. Even those
who are civilized often attend chapel wearing
one of these head-dresses, on the top of which
is mounted a man's common straw or wool hat.
The heathen women towards the interior usually
have no head-dresses, though the aged sometimes
use a small country cloth for that purpose. The
men will go without any covering for their heads
in the hottest mid-day sun ; but during the rainy
season, or at night, they are exceedingly fond

of blue and red woolen caps. They show but little foresight; if they happen to have two or three hats, perhaps they will wear them all at once, and afterwards be obliged to go without any.

The native African is extremely fond of ornaments, and the more he can obtain, the better satisfied he seems. These ornaments are of home manufacture, and often give a wild, savage look to the wearer. His arm is adorned with half a dozen large rings, made of some horny substance, perhaps the hoof of an elephant, and dotted with little bits of silver or shining steel. About his ankles are tied small scraps, called " medicines." An almost endless variety of rude chains and gree-grees hang from his neck. The leading " war-men " generally carry swords or spears, to distinguish them from others. Many of the women wear gold earrings. In short, there is no end to the fantastic decorations of the people.

Sandals are worn in West Africa to some extent. One variety is called the " *rainy season boot.*" It is made of wood, with four small
11

supports on the bottom, two or three inches in length, by means of which the foot is kept from the ground. Others are made of leather. The wearing of sandals is confined mostly to the Mohammedans. The majority of the people perform even their longest journeys barefooted.

The grotesque ideas of dress which prevail show themselves in many different ways, impossible to describe, but ridiculous in the extreme. Articles of English wear, when they can be obtained, are so mixed up with the native costume, or worn in such a ludicrous manner, as to provoke laughter. A large boy, perhaps, goes strutting round, arrayed simply in a black frock coat. A little child comes toddling after, entirely naked, except that a large straw hat is perched on his head. A heathen king, not long since, presided over a great " palaver," wearing an old red military coat with brass buttons, and a black beaver hat on his head ; otherwise, he was entirely naked.

The wealthier class of civilized natives dress in American style, and indeed nearly all the men. Some of the women wear a loose, flowing gown, called a " coverslat," which, with the prettily tied turban, forms a neat dress, well adapted to the climate. A simple shirt is the ordinary dress of school-children. In walking through the larger semi-civilized towns, a strange sight greets the eye, — a mixture of many costumes, mingling in one general stream of pedestrians. Here goes a lady in silks and muslin, and there another wrapped only in a country cloth. Yonder is a sea-captain with his broad-brimmed hat, and following him a tall Mohammedan in a flowing robe. Now we see a Christian with his Bible, and then a heathen with his gree-gree. Here is a child in full English dress, and there another entirely destitute of clothing. And so the motley throngs come and go, showing that the waves of civilization are steadily rolling in upon the country, and beating back heathen customs.

One of the first lessons a missionary is required to teach the natives here is *to dress.* The heat of the climate, and the natural indolence of the people, both unite to keep them in the old ways. Their ambition must be awak-

ened, even at the risk of its being carried too
far. There is a tendency among many who have
been surrounded by civilized influences to throw
off their clothing as soon as those influences
are withdrawn. It is a sore trial to the missionary to see those who once were neatly dressed,
relapsing into the habits of the heathen in this
respect. Nor is carelessness about dress the
only thing that pains his heart. Native converts are prone to fall in with many of the heathen customs and foolish ways. Instead of
maintaining a higher level, and drawing the
people up to them, it is too often the case that
they descend to the people. This, doubtless, is
the natural result of centuries of heathenism.
That strength of mind, energy, and ambition,
which mark the inhabitants of enlightened
lands, is not theirs; and even though the love
of God dwells in their hearts, they can not in
one or two generations rise entirely above those
degrading influences. But there is improve-
ment in this respect. Step by step, the long-
degraded sons and daughters of Africa are rising in the scale of civilization and Christianity.

The large number of languages spoken in West Africa tends to embarrass the missionary in his labors. If there was one language common to the whole coast, or even were there but a few large tribes speaking different dialects, it would be comparatively easy to give the people the gospel in their own tongue. But this is not the case. An almost unlimited number of petty tribes have each their own barbarous, unwritten language. To translate the Bible into all of these, or to become so familiar with them as to be able to preach in them, seems from experience to be hopeless. True, much has been done, and portions of the Bible have been printed in some twenty of the languages of the coast. These, however, are but a small part of the whole number. In the single city of Freetown, Sierra Leone, it is estimated that thirty different tongues are spoken. Wherever civilization and Christianity take root, the English language makes rapid advance; in fact, the native dialects, like the heathen customs, seem to die away at their approach. In many instances the books that have been published in the native tongues lie idle, while those in English are eagerly received. There are many reasons for this. One is, the people can not read at all till they are taught, and they can learn to read in English about as easily as in their own language.

Another reason is, the facility with which the African acquires a new language. He has a remarkable talent in this direction, and his wild, vagrant life, wandering from one tribe to another, and mingling almost daily with those who speak a different tongue from his own, tends to develop it. It is no uncommon thing for half-naked boatmen, who can not read a letter, to be able to speak five or six languages fluently. Father Johnson, an aged interpreter in the Mendi Mission, a native of the Kissy country far interior, is acquainted with fifteen different dialects,—among them English, Spanish, and Portuguese,—yet he can not read a word. Persons who are entirely ignorant of English, coming amid the influences of civilization, learn it in an astonishingly short time.

Doubtless there are some exceptions to these

observations. Whenever circumstances permit, as among large tribes, it is desirable that the gospel should be published and taught in the native tongue; but among most of the petty coast tribes, I am fully convinced that English will be *the* language, as Christianity advances. It is too often the case that a missionary, after spending two or three years in the country, and laboring earnestly to reduce some barbarous language to writing, is compelled by sickness to go home. Very frequently he never returns, and so his efforts are almost lost. Had the same amount of energy and toil been expended in spreading the knowledge of English, much more might have been accomplished. True, it is a pleasant sound to the churches at home to hear that the gospel has been translated into the dialect of some heathen tribe on the dark coast of West Africa; but sometimes these home reports wear a gilded covering, which the missionary on the ground can not see. Not long since, the committee of a missionary society reported to the churches that " the Word of Life was given to the people in their own language; "

while the real truth of the matter was, that, though portions of the New Testament had been translated and printed, the books lay stacked in the mission-house, scarcely one in circulation, and no desire manifested for them. The reason was, that all who could read preferred English. It is often difficult to get those who understand both English and native to read the latter. As I have said, there are exceptions; but as a general rule there are greater obstacles in the way of translating in West Africa than in most heathen countries. Of course, among all tribes, Christian natives can proclaim the gospel in their respective tongues.

The educated natives of this country speak English correctly, but those whose knowledge is limited often talk very brokenly. Indeed, to a stranger, when he first lands on these shores, it almost seems like a strange tongue, and he is disgusted with the outlandish mutilations. The dialect at Sierra Leone is known by foreigners as " Sierra Leone English," and it violates every principle of grammar and sense. It is impossible to give a true idea of it on paper, for the tones of voice and odd gestures form a prominent part. The word "sabby" is on everybody's lips, and means nearly the same as understand. If anything is not fully comprehended the reply is, "Daddy, me no sabby." If there is any dispute, it is a "palaver;" if very violent, "a big palaver." If anybody has left, the expression is, "He done gone." The word "live" is applied to all inanimate objects; thus of a cape or mountain it is said, "He live dere." If a person is particularly happy, he is "glad too much." And so, in an almost endless variety of ways, the language is tortured, till you can scarcely recognize your mother tongue. At first you are shocked; afterwards rejoiced to have even *such* a way to reach the minds and hearts of the people.

This broken English is more comprehensive in explaining spiritual ideas than most of the native languages. Some of these are sadly lacking in this respect. Nearly all of them, however, have a word for "the Great Spirit," or God. In Sherbro, he is called Hobätoke; in Mendi, Ngäwaw; in Vey, Kanabar; in Timminy,

12

Kroomassä; in Kissy, Melikä. In the Mendi language there is no word for "repent," and the people seem to have no understanding of the idea suggested by it. As a sample of West African languages, I copy the following translation of the Lord's Prayer in Sherbro, which is spoken by a tribe living on the coast between seven and eight degrees, north latitude:—

SELLEY BÄ HIH JÏSUS KRAIST LEH.

Bä hïh wunneh aiyenntokrai kōl, ïlil moa reh che shembeh. Beylï moa reh leh hoon. Jä leh moa reh che hahh'neh lehhlï reh ätōk, ken hoa leh aiyenntokrai ko'l eh. N'ka hïh nande njehmah lïh pallï. N'mai reh bon hïh len, ken'nyeh yï maia abonkoa hïh leneh. N'ma hïh reh yok kï nghel, ke n'koshï hïh jä leh woai. Halyeh Beylï leh leh hah moa eh, fossa reh, nï gbeng deh, hal chung nenen gba. Amen.

Arabic is spoken to a considerable extent among the tribes a little back from the coast. Some are able to write it, and many to read it. The Vey language, spoken by the Gallinas people, is also written.

The food of the people is simple. Rice is the "staff of life;" and without it there would soon be a famine. It forms a part, and the chief part, of every meal, when it can be obtained, which is almost always the case. Sometimes it is eaten alone, but fish and palm-oil are the two favorite accompaniments. If an African is well supplied with rice and fish, he can fare sumptuously every day. Cassada, sweet potatoes, coco, and a variety of vegetables and fruits, are also used as food, but they all occupy a subordinate place to rice. The cassada root is often beaten into flour, and then made into small round balls, called "foo-foo," which are highly prized. "Palaver sauce," made of a variety of herbs stewed in palm-oil, is one of the dainties of the country. So is the species of ant known as the "bug-a-bug," which is eagerly gathered, fried, and eaten. Cooked cats are said to be regarded as great delicacies. Lizards, snakes, and worms are sometimes used as food; and soups seasoned with certain bugs are in high repute. Much that is disgusting to civilized eyes in the way of food is constantly met with.

The time of eating is very irregular. The people commonly have but two meals in a day; the first about noon, and the last in the evening. It is an African's delight to eat a hearty meal just before going to sleep. If necessary, he can go without food for a long time, but afterwards he will be sure to make up the full quantity by inordinate stuffing. A quart of rice is the ordinary allowance for a day; and sometimes a man will save it all for the evening meal.

The modes of eating are primitive in the extreme. The table and chairs are the ground; the table-cloth, if any, a mat; the dishes, an iron pot, and perhaps a tin cup or " calabash;" the knives and forks, the fingers. It is a novel sight, at first, to witness the native meals. You are walking through a village, perhaps, and suddenly come upon a group of people squatting on the ground in a circle. Some are wrapped in country cloths; some have chalk-marked faces, and some are loaded with gree-grees. In the center of the circle stands an old iron pot, full of rice, which has just been boiled over a fire now smoldering near by. A few dried fish lic in a pan, and a gourd-shell calabash is filled with water for drinking. One after another, the people thrust their hands into the pot, and bring forth a handful of rice, which they squeeze together, and then stuff into their mouths. Now and then they pick off a piece of fish, or take a drink of water from the calabash. Meantime, they chatter away in their native tongue, and indulge in outbursts of merriment. Each one is anxious to get his share, and so the contents of the pot disappear with astonishing rapidity.

But, rude as is their mode of living, the native Africans are very hospitable. A stranger is generously lodged and supplied with food. If a man be extremely poor, he would consider it utterly beneath him to refuse to divide his rice and fish with a suffering brother. Some dwellers in Christian America might learn a lesson in this respect from the untutored heathen of West Africa.

CHAPTER VI.

HABITS — SUPERSTITION.

THE people of West Africa, like the inhabitants of every heathen country, have many habits peculiar to themselves; but I can hope only to give glimpses of a few of them. Some have been noticed in preceding chapters.

In many respects, their faults and foibles are similar to those of other heathen. The missionary's heart is often pained by the lying and dishonesty which he can not but discover. So great is the debasing power of heathenism, that even among those who give evidence of a change of heart it is difficult to instill those high-toned principles of truth and honor which ought to prevail. They can hardly believe that little evasions of truth and little acts of dishonesty are sins. Habit, like a chain, binds them to many practices over which we are compelled to cast the mantle of charity, while at the same time we seek to uproot them. Many converts, however, are bright examples of the religion of Jesus.

One marked feature in the character of this people is their great dread of reporting the misdeeds of others. They are by no means " telltales." If some wrong has been committed, and you seek to discover the perpetrator, it will sometimes require your utmost ingenuity. You may ask half a dozen, but, with the most innocent-looking faces, they will utterly deny all knowledge of the matter, while at the same time, perhaps, you are certain that they know all about it. This feeling may be partly accounted for from a fear that the reported party will revenge himself upon them, as this is a common custom. Sometimes the revenge is murder.

Foreigners are generally treated with kindness ; but if they arouse the enmity of the people the retribution is terrible. The following true story will illustrate something of the customs of the heathen, and also show the wonderful workings of Providence in raising up a missionary of the cross: —

Several years ago, one of the trading vessels which come from England to this coast chanced to stop at Taboo, a native town in the southern part of the present republic of Liberia. The captain wished to obtain a supply of palm-oil in exchange for cloths and other articles which he had brought from England. The oil was not ready for shipment, but a bargain being made with the chiefs that it should be delivered at a certain time, he very unwisely left with them a quantity of goods in payment. · The steward, named Toomey, knowing the character of the natives, remonstrated against such a course, and prophesied trouble as the result; but his suggestions were not heeded.

Having made his arrangements, the captain proceeded down the coast, and at the appointed time returned to Taboo for his oil. But, as might have been expected, no oil was to be obtained. He cruised about for some days, and at length, becoming convinced that the natives

did not intend to fulfill their agreement, he devised a plan to compel them to do so. He en-
ticed a few of the chief men on board his vessel, where he kept them as prisoners. This, of
course, greatly incensed the tribe, and they began plotting for revenge. One day, as the captain stood on deck, he saw a large number of
canoes putting off from the shore. They seemed
to contain vessels of palm-oil, and he supposed
that the agreement was about to be fulfilled.
The people brought with them a sheep and rice
for a feast, and were readily allowed to come on
board; but no sooner did they gain the deck
than a fearful scene of butchery commenced.
The captain and all the crew, with the exception of the steward, were murdered. Toomey
had fled to the hold, and hid himself under
some loose articles that were lying there.
Search was made for him, and several times
things were pulled from beneath and above him,
but he remained undiscovered. At length mos'
of the attacking party returned to the town,
leaving a few to watch the ship. The steward,
meantime, was in great agony of mind, and had

13

resolved to throw himself overboard to escape a more terrible fate; but before he could carry his resolution into effect, he was found by the guard. It seems that Toomey had previously showed them some kindnesses, and instead of killing him at once, they concluded to leave him for future disposal. So he was hurried into a canoe, with but little clothing, and taken on shore. The sun was intensely hot, and he was suffering from a high fever, and on reaching the town he asked for a drink of water, which was given him.

The chief men were soon called together to decide his fate. It is a law of the tribe that the life of those who eat and drink with them shall be held sacred. Some were for instant death; others said that as he had drunk water in their houses, he could not be killed; and so his life was spared. This poor Irish lad, who at that time did not even know the alphabet, was afterwards educated by the American Episcopal Mission at Cape Palmas, and is now the Rev. Thomas Toomey, an efficient missionary of the cross among the very people who were once almost his murderers. Truly, the ways of God are mysterious, and he makes the wrath of man to praise him.

Other instances of revenge might be related, but this is sufficient to show that although the people are kind and hospitable to strangers, their enmity if provoked is terrible.

The etiquette of the country requires strangers who visit a town to call on the king or chief, and make him some present. If this is done, the king feels bound to respect their rights while in his territory. If anything is stolen from them a " palaver " will be held, and the thief if possible discovered and punished. He also supplies them with a house, and sometimes with food. But if they neglect to bestow a present, the king is not responsible for anything that may befall them. These presents consist of various articles, such as cloth, cotton handkerchiefs, mirrors, fish-hooks, knives, and thread. As a consequence of this custom, travelers in the interior are obliged to carry with them a supply of these articles, to win the protection of the chiefs. A present costing fifty cents is gen-

erally sufficient, unless some special favor is to
be asked; but the more you give the more respect will be shown you. Foreign traders, who
wish to deal with the people in palm-oil and
the native products, are very lavish with their
presents, especially rum. But the kings understand their real character, and have not one
half of the confidence in them that they have in
the missionary, though his present may be much
smaller.

When any special favor is desired, such as
the grant of a piece of land for a trading factory or mission-house, the custom of the country
requires the purchaser to " make cananory; "
that is, the neighboring chiefs are called together in council, valuable presents are given
them, the matter is discussed with much ceremony, and the conditions of the grant decided
upon. Sometimes a full deed of the ground is
given for a certain sum of money; at others, a
yearly rent is agreed upon.

This money is usually reckoned by the " bar,"
which is equal to sixty American cents, and is
paid in articles similar to those used for pres-

ents. Gold and silver form no part of the native currency, but cloth, tobacco, rum, and all articles of trade, are known by the general name of " money." On some parts of the coast strings of a peculiar kind of shells, called " cowries," are used for money, but they form a very bulky currency, since it takes large numbers to equal the value of a penny.

If agreements are entered into with the natives, they always wish a copy of them, written on paper, which they call " book." This "book," signed by both parties, is carefully preserved, and often shown to strangers. In* the native vocabulary, everything written or printed is known by the general name of " book." If a letter is brought you, they say, " Massa, I done bring you book ; " if they wish to learn to read, it is, " Please, sir, I want to learn book."

Trading is a favorite occupation of the people, and is often carried so far as to prove a curse to the country. On the partly civilized portions of the coast there are immense numbers of petty traders, who will spend the whole day in efforts to obtain a few coppers in exchange for some

worthless article. Agriculture suffers as a
consequence, and many grovel in the deepest
poverty, who might be independent farmers.
The country people are quite skillful in trade,
and unless one is acquainted with the worth of
things, he will be likely to be cheated. The
most extravagant prices are asked for articles, — ten or twelve times as much as the seller
expects to obtain. The missionary is obliged
to trade with them, and his patience is often
severely taxed in concluding a bargain.

It is difficult to get a clear idea of the religious
belief of the natives of this country ; indeed, it
may be said that they have no clear ideas of the
subject themselves. They offer their little sacrifices, and perform their ceremonies, more
blindly than the heathen in many other parts
of the world. They seem to adhere to their
" customs " simply because it is the fashion of
their country, and not from a clear understanding of the object. Superstition reigns over
them, and shapes their actions. They grope
blindly in its mazes, degraded, crushed, bewil-
dered.

The worship of idols of wood and stone is not common on the immediate coast, though it prevails to some extent. The remains of several stone idols were found a few years ago at Mo Tappan, one of the stations of the Mendi Mission, exhibiting various forms of disease in the human body. It is supposed that they were worshiped by persons afflicted with such diseases. I have sometimes thought that this field would be more hopeful if idol-worship prevailed, for then the people would see more clearly the importance of being faithful in *some* religion. But though they do not bow down to wood and stone, they are still none the less heathen. We see their superstition in a hundred forms. They believe in a multitude of "spirits," to whom they offer sacrifices for the purpose of appeasing their wrath or obtaining some favor. These spirits are supposed to reside in the trees, rocks, mountains, rivers, and bug-a-bug hills, and to have different kinds of power. The offerings consist of rice, palm-oil, cloth, tin cups, or almost any article which the person has. If these sacrifices chance to be eaten by animals, or removed for any cause, it is thought that the spirit has accepted them. The curious bug-a-bug hills, before described, seem to be favorite residences of the spirits; and in traveling through the country it is very common to see a piece of cloth or a tin cup lying upon them.

Many of the people have a great fear of these spirits. Near one of the American mission stations of this coast there stands a large cotton-tree, which the neighboring heathen imagine to be the abode of one of them. Its peculiar care is supposed to be to keep watch over the mission-house and protect it. They believe that if anything is stolen, the spirit will punish the thief. As a consequence of this superstition, mission property is safe; and on one occasion some articles which were stolen were returned, so great was the fear of the spirit's displeasure.

While journeying up the rivers, I once passed a mountain which is said to be the residence of a great war-spirit, called Kasilon. Warriors about to undertake an expedition against an adjoining tribe often make a pilgrimage to this mountain, and profess to hold communion with the spirit, after which they regard themselves as invincible. It is supposed, however, that those who talk with Kasilon, though they may gather strength for a time, can not live long.

Our old interpreter tells me the following story of superstition among the Kissy people, who live towards the interior. In one part of their country there is a small mountain, where they believe a spirit dwells, who seems from the story to hold the "horn of plenty." No one cultivates the mountain land, yet there is said to be a never-failing supply of corn, coco, yams, plantain, oranges, potatoes, and every kind of food, including meat. The spirit rules over all, and deals it out with a bountiful hand on certain conditions. If a person wishes for oranges, for instance, he may go to the mountain and gather basket after basket till he is satisfied; but if he chance to touch the coco or yam, the spirit gets angry, and gives him a severe flogging. So, if he wishes yams, he may gather any quantity of them, but must not touch anything else. Only one thing can be

14

taken at a time, but that may be had in abundance. On the bank of a small stream which
flows down the mountain there is an immense
rock, which is worshiped by the people. Cows
are sometimes killed and offered in sacrifice to
it. The old man who related this story to me
is a Christian, yet such is the power of heathen
habits that he seemed half inclined to believe
in this wonderful spirit of the mountain.

It is a common custom in West Africa to offer sacrifices to the dead. In some places, if a
king or noted man dies, a number of slaves are
at once killed, so that, as they say, he may be
supplied with servants in the other world. The
people seem to have no idea of the nature of
spirits, but think that they eat and drink like
mortal beings. Friends will lay rice and palm-
oil on the graves of the dead, saying, " They
are hungry, and we must feed them ;" and it
is difficult to make them believe that the spirits
do not really eat those articles. A native missionary was once journeying up one of the rivers of the coast, and being kindly treated by a
man at one of the towns at which he stopped,

he presented him with a small tin cup. The missionary continued his journey, and in returning called at the same town. What was his surprise to find that the man had laid the new cup on his father's grave as a sacrifice, and was again using an old, leaky "calabash" to drink from. The missionary remonstrated, and told him that he did not give him the cup for any such purpose, but in vain ; the only reply was, "My father needs it more than I, and he shall have it." It was all superstition ; yet this poor heathen man, in his blindness and degradation, exhibited a filial affection, and a devotion to what he believed was right, that would put to shame many a professing Christian.

Although the worship of graven images does not prevail to any great extent on the immediate coast, still the people are idolaters. Almost every heathen village has its "idol houses," sometimes called "country-fashion houses" or "devil houses." Sacrifices are offered and a certain degree of worship paid to them. No idol, in the common acceptation of the word, however, is to be seen. These houses are commonly built in a circular form, some two or three feet in hight, and one and a half in diameter, and covered with a little pointed roof of thatch. Underneath this, on the ground, are laid a variety of small articles, such as sticks, shells, pieces of broken crockery, spires from bug-a-bug hills, and bits of cloth. I incline to the belief that these articles are not themselves worshiped, but that they are regarded as sacred offerings to some spirit who is supposed to have his residence in the idol house. Be that as it may, the articles seen are very insignificant. I have never noticed among them any unbroken pieces of crockery, but invariably worthless remnants. The people seem to think that the wrath of spirits or idols, whatever they are, is easily appeased. In walking through a village, you will often see these idol houses standing near the residences of the principal men. Sometimes they are built around a bug-a-bug hill, in the outskirts of the town.

In some towns there are also heathen altars,

intended for the offering of sacrifices. Their construction is very simple. Four sticks of wood are laid on the ground, so as to enclose a space of a few square feet. This is slightly elevated above the surrounding earth, and the offerings are laid upon it. I well remember preaching in a heathen town towards the interior, with one of these altars in full sight, and but a few feet from where I stood. Indeed, the missionary has frequent occasion to use the precise language of Paul in his sermon on Mars Hill, which so plainly describes the state of the heathen here. " In all things " they " are too superstitious," and they worship they know not what.

" Gree-grees," charms, and " medicines" are universally worn by the people of West Africa, and the people's faith in them is very great. The infant, almost as soon as born, is loaded with them, and the old man tottering towards the grave trusts in them. They are made in different forms, and worn for a variety of purposes. A common form of the gree-gree consists of a string of leather or palm fiber, from

which is suspended a small, flat package, either
oblong or square, containing the charm. This
kind of gree-gree is usually worn around the
neck. Other "medicines" are worn on the
arms, the wrists, the waist, the ankles and feet,
the ears, and sometimes tied to a corner of the
clothing. There is a class of persons known as
gree-gree makers, who are supposed to have supernatural powers. If a person desires a charm,
he applies to a gree-gree man, telling him the
purpose for which he wishes it, and the article
is duly manufactured. One kind of "medicine"
is supposed to protect the wearer from the as-
saults of enemies; another, to deliver him from
danger when journeying by water; another, to
make him a rapid walker if traveling by land;
another, to prevent serpents from biting him;
others, to keep off various diseases; and still
others answer a great variety of objects. If a
house is to be plundered, "medicine" is put
upon it which is believed to have the power of
causing the inmates to fall into so deep a sleep
as not to be awakened by the thieves. If a
man wishes to revenge himself upon his enemy,

he repeats a form of words each day over a
gree-gree obtained for the purpose, with the belief that it will cause him to sicken and die.
So great is the power of superstition that if a
gree-gree is tied about a fruit tree, the people
will not dare to touch the fruit; or if " medicine " is placed in the farm, the yams, corn and
potatoes are comparatively safe. Among many
of the heathen the gree-gree seems to be the
universal remedy for and defense against the
ills of life. The missionary, in combating
these varied forms of superstition, feels ready
to exclaim, —

> " Who, but thou, Almighty Spirit,
> Can the heathen world reclaim?
> Men may preach, but till thou favor
> Heathens will be still the same."

CHAPTER VII.

WE naturally expect a superstitious people to be firm believers in witchcraft. This is certainly true of the natives of West Africa. A belief in witches underlies the whole structure of society, and leads to many revolting customs and deeds of cruelty. Even those who have become christianized can hardly dispel from their minds the lingering relics of this superstition; but among the heathen it is seen in all its sickening and terrible aspects. Many human lives are yearly sacrificed to it, the poor victims often undergoing the most cruel tortures that heathen minds can devise, before death comes to their relief.

Witchcraft is supposed to be the cause of almost everything bad. If a person is caught by

112

a shark or an alligator, killed by a leopard, or meets with any accident, it is attributed to a witch, and efforts are at once made to discover the guilty party. The proceedings to effect this object doubtless vary in different places. Among the Sherbro people it is accomplished through " country-fashion men," who pretend to a supernatural power and wisdom, which enable them to point out a witch.

The " country-fashion man " first proceeds to the town where supposed witchcraft has been practised, informs the king of his object, and promises certainly to detect the culprit. The king pledges him a certain amount of money in case he succeeds. A large fire is then built in the town, and the people summoned to sit around it. The occasion is made as imposing as possible. The " country-fashion man " assumes an air of great wisdom, and goes through with a variety of incantations and strange ceremonies, so as to awe the people. He holds in his hand a gree-gree, in the shape of a rod, which he flourishes wildly during the ceremony. Suddenly he strikes one of the group with this gree-

15

gree rod, the touch of which is an accusation of witchcraft, and then goes on with his wild performance, till he is satisfied that no more witches remain.

Next comes the trial, which is conducted with more ceremony than the accusation. The mode commonly adopted is known as the "*sassy-wood trial.*" The country-fashion man goes to a sassy-wood tree, plunges a needle and knife into the trunk, and addresses it something as follows: "O tree, I beseech you to decide truly whether or not the person about to be tried is guilty." He next cuts off a quantity of bark, beats it to a fine pulp in a mortar, and makes a sort of tea from it. No other individual is allowed to touch the bark during its preparation, lest he should take from it its supposed power. A kind of scaffold is now built, and the accused placed upon it in a standing posture. The people sit upon the ground around the scaffold in large numbers, every eye fixed on the victim. The operator dips up a calabash of tea, and administers it; then, after a pause, another, and another. If the accused does not vomit the tea, he is deemed guilty, and punished by death. If, however, he vomits freely, he is taken from the scaffold and placed on country cloths; but if he now chances to throw up bloody matter, he is still regarded as guilty; if not, he is set at liberty.

The modes of inflicting the death-punishment are various. Sometimes, after waiting a sufficient time for the sassy-wood to operate, the people commence beating the victim with sticks and stones, and continue it till he is dead. In other cases he is roasted alive, undergoing the most exquisite tortures, till death comes to his relief. A few years ago, in a village near one of the stations of the Mendi Mission, three women who had been found guilty of witchcraft were punished by burning. Crotches were driven into the ground, and sticks laid across them. The victims were stretched upon these sticks and bound, with their backs downward. Slow fires were kept burning underneath, and the women left to their fate. Rumors of their awful position reached the mission, and one of the missionaries hastened to their rescue. They were brought away, but two of them died in a few days. In this same village a young girl was once convicted of witchcraft, and sentenced to die. She was tied to a stake at low water, so that as the tide rose it would overwhelm and drown her. By some means she got loose, and returned to the town ; she was then taken to an adjoining island, stabbed, and her body thrown into the river. This record of cruelties practised in one small village is but a sample of those carried on throughout a vast extent of country.

The people, of course, have many strange ideas concerning the so-called witches. Some of the Sherbro tribe believe the following curious story : The witch is said to have a large six-oared canoe, which he securely anchors, not on the surface of the water, but at the bottom. He then assumes the shape of an alligator, and swims about in search of prey. If he catches a man, woman, or child, he descends to the canoe anchored at the bottom of the river, and leaves his victim there. He next spends several days in swimming about in his alligator disguise, passing near all the neighboring towns, and listening at each to hear what the people say. If he hears nothing said about the person who has been caught, he will return to the witch-canoe and devour him; but if he sees that the people "make palaver" and talk of the sassy-wood trial, he will bring the victim back unharmed. A multitude of similar stories, as wild as they are inconsistent, are repeated among the people, and believed to a greater or less extent.

West Africa, though a heathen land, has its secret societies. One of the most powerful of these is denominated the "Purrow," and exerts a wonderful influence over the people. Its members consist of men only, and each one is bound by a solemn oath not to reveal anything concerning its secret ceremonies. Death would doubtless be the penalty for a violation of this oath, which is so strictly kept that those who are not members can never obtain a full knowledge of the proceedings.

The sessions of the purrow are usually held in a large forest, or "bush," as it would be denominated in Africa, at some distance from any

town or village. The same spot is kept for this
purpose from year to year, and is regarded as
sacred by the people. Outsiders are rigidly
excluded from the vicinity; and if, during a
session of the purrow, a woman chances to approach the bush, the penalty is death. Nearly
all the kings of the country belong to the society, and none of them dare dispute its edicts.

There is one chief " devil " in the purrow,
called " Tassaw," who acts as a sort of modera-
tor. All, even the kings, fear him, and doubtless many regard him as a supernatural being.
There are also several minor " devils," all of
whom are men dressed in hideous costume.
The Tassaw wears an immense gree-gree on
his head, composed of human skulls, bones, &c.
His body is covered with platted bamboo fiber,
and a net-work of bones from human skeletons.
His face is rubbed with the ashes of a human
being, and he inspires great terror among the
superstitious people.

There is a secret society also among the
women, called the " Boondoo," which answers
much the same purpose among them as the

purrow among the men. Its secrets, strange to say, are kept as profoundly.

" Cries " for the dead are very common among the heathen of West Africa. The missionary, as he enters a town, often hears wild moans and wailings issuing from some one of the little mud huts. Friends gather round the corpse, and give vent to their grief in loud lamentations. Sometimes they utter expressions of regret for the departed, and praise his virtues. One moment the cries rise loud, harsh and discordant, and the next they sink to the softest and most plaintive moans. Occasionally, the mourners tear their hair, cut their flesh, and toss about in a frightful manner. The length of the cry depends on various circumstances; for a powerful king it might last a year; for a common person, only a week, in both cases being continued at intervals. Hired mourners are sometimes employed to cry for the dead, in which case they feign the deepest grief, and carry on their operations in the most extravagant manner. At the burial, the cries are often heart-rending.

Polygamy is generally practiced among this people; in fact, almost every heathen man who is able has a plurality of wives. A man's property is often measured by the number of them which he possesses. The women are purchased from their parents or friends for a small sum, sometimes not more than three or four dollars. They are not themselves consulted in the matter, but when bargained for, willing or unwilling, must go. Prince Mannah, a noted Gallinas king, living a few miles from the Mendi Mission, is said to have a thousand wives. Some of them he does not even know by sight. In a civilized country the cost of supporting so many would forbid the custom, if there were no other reasons; but here the tables are turned, and the wives support their husband. They perform the drudgery, while their lord sits at ease in his hammock, and issues his orders.

A curious custom prevails among some of the West African tribes in regard to the wives of a dead king. During the days of mourning they are closely watched, and not suffered to go out alone; but on the morning on which the cry is ended, they are all taken to the river to bathe. Those who wish to secure them as wives follow, and at a point higher up the river throw short sticks into the water, which float down to the women. If a woman chooses to accept the proposal of marriage, she picks up the stick; if not, she allows it to float by.

Poisoning is a common mode of revenge in Africa. The people are very superstitious in regard to it, believing that their enemies are possessed of various subtile poisons, which remain for a long time in the system, but finally kill. Those who prepare food for the kings and chiefs are required to taste of every dish, as a sort of pledge that no poison has been mixed with it. But notwithstanding all precautions, many lives are doubtless taken every year by these means.

The Mohammedan religion prevails to some extent in West Africa, and portions of the Koran are in circulation. The Mohammedans are generally possessed of superior minds, but practice great impositions on the heathen. Some can read and write Arabic with much facility,

16

and a few schools are established in the larger
towns.   They are much more difficult to reach
with the gospel than the purely heathen.   The
common people purchase from them gree-grees
and charms, and sometimes regard them with a
sort of reverence because they are " book " or
" murray men."

CHAPTER VIII.

THE centuries of darkness that have rolled over Africa have left upon it indelible marks. Its skies are as smiling as ever, its breezes as odorous, its flowers as gorgeous, its fruits as luscious, and its vegetation as luxuriant; but the blight and mildew of those dark ages rest heavily over the people. Like all heathen nations, they are blinded and ignorant, warped by superstition, and swayed by fear and passion. They exhibit much natural talent, which if developed and guided might make them a great power in the world. Even in their degraded state, there are many instances of native nobleness and commanding strength of mind that can not but inspire respect from all.

These traits of character are all seen in the government of the country. Some kings and chiefs rule with a dignified bearing and firm hand, really striving to do good to their subjects; but, inwoven with the good, there is much of superstition and cruelty. The large number of petty tribes on the West African coast renders any general form of government impossible, though there is considerable similarity in the regulations enforced. The purrow is the source of many general laws, which the kings are bound to respect; otherwise war is made upon them. With this exception, each king is independent, and can manage his own towns and villages as he chooses. The people usually show much respect to their kings, and obey them with alacrity.

If any disagreement is to be settled, a " palaver" is called. These palavers are usually held in the barre, or court-house, of the town, and the king of the place presides at them. Quite a number of people often assemble to listen. The parties bring forward their witnesses and present their pleas, and the king with his counselors sits in state, hearing the case, and finally decides as is deemed just. The palavers are conducted with much dignity and ceremony. Some of the speeches are really eloquent, at least so far as the outside appearance goes. I have sat in a palaver-house in African wilds, listening to the speakers as they poured forth a torrent of words in their native tongue, till my heart has been fairly thrilled. I know not what they were saying, but the commanding figure, the erect and manly bearing, the graceful, speaking gestures, the face lit up with the inspiration of the moment, and the softly-modulated voice, made an impression scarcely inferior to that of the popular orators of civilized lands. The decisions of the palaver are not always what they should be, for heathen superstitions and cruelties are mixed up with every form of justice. Often the palavers are brought to the missionary for decision, and much of his precious time and strength is taken up in listening, through an interpreter, to the various statements. In such cases, his verdict is cheerfully accepted by both parties as final.

Unadjusted palavers between different tribes often lead to those petty wars which are always prevailing to a greater or less extent on this coast. The cause of war is commonly some trifling matter, scarcely worth noticing at all, which is dwelt upon and magnified, till the king and people are roused to the requisite pitch for an attack. Indeed, many kings seem to delight in war, for the sake of the spoils and prisoners which they hope to capture.

The forces employed are usually quite small, perhaps two or three hundred on a side. They are armed with old-fashioned muskets, swords of native manufacture, and some other weapons. Some towns are defended with small cannon, obtained from traders. The attacking party approach a town with a stealthy, cat-like tread, skulking among bushes and hiding behind trees, so as to surprise the people if possible. Strategetic movements are much more popular with African soldiers than a hand-to-hand conflict; but when necessary they fight with a desperate bravery. The swift movements and sudden attacks of African war-parties are surprising. At

sunset a village reposes in quiet beauty amid
its groves of graceful palms and bending cocoas.
The log canoe of the rude fisherman glides
peacefully homeward over the river. The people gather in barre and kitchen for their evening chat. Not the faintest signs of an approaching enemy are discernible on land or
water. Darkness comes on, and suddenly at
the midnight hour the fierce war-cry of a foe
is heard. The thatched huts are ablaze. The
terrified inhabitants, not prepared to resist, fly
for their lives. Many are taken prisoners,
plunder is secured, and then the enemy departs
as suddenly as he came. The morning sun
shines on blackened ruins and deserted homes,
where but yesterday the simple round of heathen life went on in fancied security.

One object of these wars is to obtain slaves ;
nearly all the prisoners captured being regarded as such. But slavery in West Africa is
very different from the bondage practiced by
some civilized nations. The master and slave
are of the same color, though usually of different tribes. They are both ignorant and super-

stitious, and are regarded as more nearly equals in their privileges than the masters and slaves of America. One might pass through towns where there are hundreds of slaves, and yet never suspect that the institution existed there at all. The usual title of the slaveholder is "father," and his treatment of his slaves generally warrants this name. Slaves are allowed to acquire property of their own, and if they are diligent and faithful they may become the richest men in the country. They often own slaves themselves, who are sent out to work for the masters in their stead. Many sad wrongs, however, spring out of the institution in this modified state, and as civilization and Christianity advance it gradually fades away.

Many of the slaves of this country are stolen from their parents while young. A mother, for instance, sends her child to a spring for water, and he never returns. The woods may echo to her anguished cries, but he comes not. Kidnappers were lurking in the bush, and suddenly they pounced upon their prey, and bore him off. Others are stolen while going on some errand, or playing about the village. Men are often prowling about in the dense bush which surrounds the native towns, watching for their victims. Father Johnson, the old interpreter of the Mendi Mission, was stolen from his native country, far interior, by these kidnappers. He was then some eight years of age, and had been sent by his mother to a town at some distance to visit his older brother. While passing the bush, three men suddenly pounced upon him, and bore him off. They traveled by night, and hid in the bush during the day, until at length they reached the Gallinas country, and the victim was sold as a slave. Father Johnson has never seen his parents or relatives since. Often the child is so young when stolen that he has no remembrance of his country or people. The method of obtaining slaves, and the mode of treating them, vary somewhat among different tribes. On the east of Calabar, hundreds of miles below Sierra Leone, lies the country of the Fellatahs, one of the southern provinces of Luccatoo. The inhabitants are described as fierce men, who ride on horseback.

17

They are Mohammedans, and by their con-
quests reduce many to slavery, and sell them to
other tribes. In some places there are laws,
the breaking of which is punished by slavery.
Sometimes, if a person is accused of witchcraft,
and successfully passes the sassy-wood ordeal,
his accuser is sold as a slave. Among some
tribes, if a man owes more than he is able to
pay, he is sold to make up the balance. A
missionary at Calabar relates the following
story of a device that is practiced for obtaining
slaves : —

" The Ibo tribe believe in a being whom they
call *Tshuku*, and whose shrine is at Aro, a town
lying west of this, in the Delta. People go thither from surrounding tribes to consult this ora-
cle, and it is held in high repute. The pilgrim
carries his present with him. The place where
the priests meet him is said to be outside of the
town of Aro, where there is a house built over
a small stream. If the present is deemed satis-
factory, the pilgrim is sent back with his answer.
But many never return from that house. It is
believed that Tshuku has devoured them. In

order to give color to this deception, a red dye, or perhaps at times real human blood, is spilled in the stream, and is seen by those outside."

The foreign slave-trade is still carried on to some extent from West Africa, though the number of slaves exported has greatly diminished during the past few years. The Sherbro country, in the vicinity of the Mendi Mission, was formerly a great resort of slave-ships, and many are the dark tales of blood and crime related concerning them. The numerous rivers and mangrove islands afforded them great opportunities to carry on the wicked traffic with comparative safety. It is impossible to conceive the fearful deeds of cruelty and the sickening horrors that attended it. If the secret history of the foreign slave-trade from West Africa could be written, it would fill volumes with the most thrilling pictures of human agony and woe, exceeding in strangeness and mystery the wildest dreams that ever entered the head of a novelist. God be praised that those dark days of terror are so fast passing away.

CHAPTER IX.

THE WORK OF MISSIONS.

EVER since our Saviour's last command, "Go ye into all the world and preach the gospel to every creature," his church has been engaged, to a greater or less extent, in the work of missions. The story of salvation through Christ, which was then known only in the region immediately surrounding Jerusalem, has been spread far and wide. Heathen Europe heard the sound and awoke to life. It crossed the Atlantic with the Pilgrims, and Christian America to-day testifies to its wondrous power. Great things have been accomplished, too, in these later times by the spread of the gospel through the instrumentality of missions. Missionaries have been sent forth into many of the dark places of the earth. With a silent, patient heroism, daunted not by the prospect of danger, or even of death, they have sundered the ties that bound them to friends and native land, and buried themselves in foreign wilds, surrounded only by untamed men. They have trod the burning sands of Africa, and journeyed over its sluggish, death-breeding rivers. They have penetrated its jungles and visited its kraals. They have braved the fierce cold and eternal snows of Greenland. They have visited the crowded cities and villages of India. They have combated the false beliefs of many an Asiatic nation. They have gone to the most lonely islands of the ocean. And everywhere they have told the same sweet story of redeeming love, and besought the heathen to accept of Christ. And not only have men done this, but gentle woman, tenderly nurtured, and surrounded by the luxuries of a civilized land, has joyfully forsaken all, and borne a noble part in the blessed work.

The results of the missionary work are already grand and glorious. The wilderness and the desert are budding and blossoming. Many isles of the sea have become christianized, and

dark corners of the earth lit up with the rays
of the Sun of Righteousness. Souls are rejoicing in glory to-day who have been saved through
this instrumentality. No tongue can fully utter, and no pen fully describe, the wonderful
results which, through God's blessing, have followed the labors of his servants in foreign lands.
Even in West Africa, though the deadly climate
necessitates a frequent change of laborers, much
·progress has been made. There is a line of
missions extending for thousands of miles along
the coast, while here and there stations have
been planted in the interior. From these the
gospel light is constantly radiating ; and wherever it is shed, the superstitions and ceremonies
of heathenism are fast passing away. Already
there are many thousands of native converts,
and from among them some educated pastors
and teachers are employed in the regular mission work.

From day to day the progress is scarcely discernible, but glancing back over a series of
years, it becomes very apparent. The work
does go forward, though to mortal eyes the ad-

vance may seem very slow. Missionary life in West Africa is not without its shady side. Oppressed with the languor peculiar to a tropical climate, enfeebled by the ever-recurring fever, with his nervous system unstrung, and a crowd of duties constantly calling for attention, the missionary's heart sometimes sinks within him. As he looks over the field, where for months and years he has toiled, and sees so little fruit, he is ready to exclaim, "What good have I accomplished by all these labors?" That delightful vail of romance, which, perchance, surrounded the foreign missionary work when he looked at it from his old New England home, has long ago departed. It is a stern, matter-of-fact reality now, yet the work itself is far more dear than ever. Those fancy pictures, which the good folks at home so delight to draw, of a missionary sitting all day under a branching tree, with a group of eager, earnest learners about him, are not always realized. He must sometimes gather the naked, filthy children, and wash and clothe them. He must seek out the people in their dark, damp huts, and converse

with them there. He must gaze on disgusting
objects every day, and feel his soul pained by
heathen habits. He must repeat over and over
the simplest truths of the gospel, and then sometimes fail of making them plain to the darkened
mind. But the joys of the work far outbalance
the petty trials and discouragements. The missionary realizes that

> " The lonely heart that leans on God
>   Is happy anywhere ; "

and, though conscious of his own weakness, he
is strong in the Lord. He knows that he is
entirely dependent on the Holy Spirit; but he
knows, too, that that Spirit has been promised
him. Turning over the pages of my missionary
journal, I find many a record speaking of these
things : —

Dec. 5. — God fulfills to us his precious promise, that whosoever forsaketh houses or lands,
or father or mother, for Jesus' sake, shall receive a hundred fold more in this life. " Lo, I
am with you always ! " has been blissfully veri-
fied in our experience. Trials, to be sure, have
pressed upon us, and we have been ofttimes in

great perplexity, scarcely knowing which way to turn; yet over and through all has gleamed the sunshine of God's face and the smile of his love. We expect these trials, for Jesus said that the " hundred fold " would be accompanied " with persecutions " here, but sweet, very sweet, are the anticipations of " everlasting life " beyond.

Doubtless, many who seem to listen gladly soon forget our words; but we trust that God opens the hearts of some to receive permanent good. It is ours to sow the seed wherever we can, God's to give the increase; and we have no right to believe that any labor for Jesus will be utterly in vain. The harvest may be long delayed, and the reapers few and unworthy; but never was there a word spoken nor suffering patiently endured for Christ's sake in vain. Often in our work, as we long and pray for the delaying harvest, we feel ready to exclaim, —

" Full well I know I have more tares than wheat, —
 Brambles and flowers, dry sticks, and withered leaves;
Wherefore I blush and weep, and at thy feet
I kneel down reverently and repeat,
 " Master, behold my sheaves.

18

I know these blossoms, clustering heavily,
  With evening dew upon their folded leaves,
Can claim no value or utility ;
  Yet well I know thy patient love perceives
Not what I did, but what I strove to do,
And, though the full, ripe ears be sadly few,
  Thou wilt accept my sheaves.''

Many faithful missionaries have been called
to seal their testimony for Jesus with their lives
on heathen ground. Their burial-places are
consecrated spots, rendered for ever sacred by
the dust of fallen laborers. The West African
coast is lined with these sad memorials. Some
had but just been permitted to lift the banner
of the cross ere they fell in death. But not
one has fallen in vain. Silent voices come
forth from their grass-grown graves, speaking
of a high and lofty faith, a noble zeal, a wil-
lingness to die if need be, only that they might
have the sweet privilege of pointing heathen to
the cross of Christ. Parents, and brothers,
and sisters, may have wept bitterly over the
loved ones early called, and almost felt that the
sacrifice for Africa's redemption was too great ;
but our dear heavenly Father saw it all, and
will overrule it to the glory of his kingdom.

CHAPTER X.

MUCH of the labor of missionaries may well be denominated *wayside teaching.* Wherever a group of listeners can be found or gathered, there an opportunity is offered of doing good, and the faithful missionary will be ready to embrace it. I extract the following notes from my journal : —

Dec. 21.—God commands us to *go* to every creature with the offer of salvation, and if we can not find them elsewhere we must visit them at their homes. Let me picture one of these visits.—It is towards evening, and putting my small Testament in my pocket, I start on my walk. Passing through our pleasant yard and out at the gateway, I find myself in one of the main roads of the region. Americans would call it a mere foot-path, but in this wagonless country it is all the road we have. On one side is the Sherbro river, some five miles in width, and dotted with numerous mangrove islands, and on the other the lime-hedge that bounds our mission grounds. People are constantly coming and going along the path. Here is a tall Mohammedan, wearing a flowing white cloth reaching from his shoulders to the ground, and adorned with rings of ivory and gold about his wrists and arms. He wears a country gree-gree round his neck, which is supposed to keep off evil spirits. He is followed by some women, with their faces curiously marked with white chalk. Yonder, on the river-bank, is a group of naked boys and girls. Others, queerly dressed, are passing by. Walking a little distance along this path, I turn up a shady lane, and soon reach the native village of Gondamar. The houses are small, with mud walls and thatched roofs, and are scattered promiscuously about. Near one of the houses a small girl is beating rice in a mortar, and several women stand around her. I pass up to them, and speak in English. They all laugh aloud, and shake their heads. They are Sherbro people, and can understand nothing that I say. Soon another woman comes up, and says a few words in broken English. I talk with her a while about Jesus, invite her to come to the chapel on Sunday, and then pass on.

I next stop at the door of a country house. It looks dark inside. There is no floor but the bare earth, and only two rooms. A fire is burning in the middle of one room, and over it a pot of rice is suspended. A man comes forward and meets me. He talks English quite fluently, and I can speak to him with much more ease about his soul. As I leave, he thanks me for what I have said. Next I visit the chief of the town. He brings a low stool, and places it outside the door for me to sit upon ; and as I converse with him about the Bible, and read from it some passages, a group gathers round us. Leaving the chief's house, I stop at other huts, or say a few words to those whom I meet. Near the farther end of the village, I find an old woman who lived in Sierra Leone, and attended chapel there years ago. She welcomes me gladly, and I read a chapter from the Testament as I sit by her mud house. A half-dozen others crouch on the ground around me, gazing earnestly into my face. So I pass from house to house, trying to point souls to Jesus, until the evening shadows begin to fall, when I turn homewards.

Dec. 23.—Monday evening I took another "wayside walk" to a heathen village. James, one of our mission boys, went with me to interpret. We found two or three men standing near one of the houses, and I commenced talking with them about God. Soon, nearly a dozen, attracted by our conversation, gathered around to hear. Some of them were Mohammedans, or "murray-men," as they are called, from the interior, and could read Arabic. After conversing with these for a while, we called at the doors of several houses, and tarried for a few moments to speak of Jesus: and so, walking from place to place, and carrying the good tidings, we reached some whom we could not otherwise have gained access to. In one part

of the village we found some country people, who said they had never heard a missionary talk about God; and calling James to interpret, I spent ten minutes, as long a time as they would attentively listen at once, in repeating the story of the cross. They gave good attention to the word spoken. As the twilight shadows gathered, we returned to the mission-house.

June 17.—Shall I give you a little sketch of mission life to-day? It may afford a glimpse of one of the many features of our work.

It is a clear, hot morning, and the tropical sun is already high in the heavens. As usual, I am to spend two or three hours with a group of learners in the barre at Bonthe, a native town three-fourths of a mile distant. The path by land is so wet and miry that I am obliged to go on the water. Passing down to our little wharf, I step into my log canoe. I sit on a stool near the prow, and a man at the stern paddles. The canoe is some twelve feet long, and one and a half wide, hollowed out of a single log. As we glide along, it sways this way

and that, the upper edge often nearly even with
the water. A frightened person would be sure
to upset it, and as the river is full of sharks and
alligators, that might prove no light matter.
On one side is the island shore, with its small
brown huts and a few palms rising against the
sunlit sky; on the other is the broad Sherbro
river, with canoes of all sizes and shapes, filled
with dusky, half-naked people, gliding in every
direction. Naked children play along the beach,
and men and women, with a strip of cloth wound
around their waists, walk to and fro, or lounge
in the sun. The faces and bodies of many of
the women are grotesquely marked with white
chalk. Twenty minutes' paddling brings me to
Bonthe. A short walk over a strip of burning
sand and along the winding paths of the town,
and I find myself in the chief's yard, bounded on
three sides by the barre, kitchen, and house, and
on the fourth by a rude fence. The children
crowd round me as I enter, and three or four
little hands are placed in mine at once, with a
broken " Mornin', sir ! " from a score of voices.
At first they were frightened at the sight of a

white man, but now they are very familiar.
Many understood no English when they came,
but they soon learn to talk. It requires considerable planning to gather the children, and sometimes a little force. I see a boy, for instance,
playing about the town, and send a couple of
the older children to invite him to the barre.
He is frightened at the bare idea, and runs off
screaming. They pursue, and after a short
chase come back panting with the boy in their
arms. He screams and kicks furiously, but
one holds him while the other puts on a shirt,
and they bear him in triumph to the barre. I
lay my hand on his head and speak gently, and
he is soothed; and in a few days, perhaps, he
becomes a quiet, constant learner.

The barre has a thatched roof, mud floor,
and mud walls on three sides, the fourth
being open. Rude seats are ranged around
the walls, on which the learners sit, and a table
and chair are provided for me. At a stroke of
the bell I read a few verses from the Bible, and
we kneel in prayer. Then follows the patience-
trying work of teaching the elements of read-
19

ing and spelling to a group of heathen.   Printed tablets hang on the walls, and as the class
gather around them, eager and attentive, the
scene is interesting.   Some have already learned
to read short sentences, and repeat easy verses
from the Scriptures.   As I tell them about God,
their eyes open with wonder.   A few can not
yet understand my English words.   When the
little ones, so lately in heathenism, recite such
lines as, " Suffer little children to come unto
me," " Now I lay me down to sleep," &c., my
heart overflows with thanksgiving.   There are
often several grown men who come to be taught,
so that the classes as they stand before the tablets vary from the full-sized man to the toddling
child.

The group in the barre is a never-ceasing object of curiosity to those without.   A much
frequented path leads past the building, and the
passers-by often stop and watch us eagerly, chat
in their native tongue, and laugh.   Some come
within the yard, and, hiding themselves behind
a mud wall, peer round the corner with gaping
mouth and wide-open eyes.   The kitchen oppo-

site is full of loungers. A heathen woman brings a tub of water, sets it down in front of the barre, and proceeds to wash her children, the little sufferers meanwhile screaming at the top of their voices. Having done this, she stripes their shining black faces and bodies with white chalk, adorns them with rings, gree-grees, and little tinkling bells, and sends them off to play. Another woman brings her crying children, and seats herself on the edge of the barre. A tall Mohammedan from the interior, adorned with unnumbered rings, " medicines," and charms, pauses and sits down. Three or four others join the group, and all watch us as though it were a show.

But listen to that noise. A " boondoo " procession is passing. It consists of a dozen women, who keep up a constant song or chant. Sometimes they walk along, singing, clapping their hands, and shaking a gourd covered with loose beads; sometimes they go on a sort of half-run, giving now and then a deafening shout. They are dressed in cloths wound round their bodies, and adorned with heathen ornaments.

Amid such scenes the hours pass, and at the close we kneel and repeat together the Lord's Prayer, which many have learned. The children crowd round me with smiling faces, and a dozen hands are held out at once, while " Good-by, sir!" echoes from every side. A few follow me to the wharf, and watch me as I glide homeward in my light canoe.

CHAPTER XI.

EC. 21.—Yesterday, after the morning
service in the chapel, I went to a little village a half-mile distant to preach. Horace
accompanied me. We walked along a narrow path through a mangrove swamp, which is
overflowed at high tide. The water was low as
we passed, and by jumping across an occasional
pool we succeeded in reaching the village.
There were not more than ten houses in the
place, and the people did not understand English. We could not find a tree large enough
to hold the meeting under it, and so the people
gathered in the shade of one of the mud-walled
huts. We began with singing, and then Horace read the seventh chapter of Matthew in
Sherbro, and I offered prayer through an in-

terpreter. Next I spoke for a short time about Christ and our need of salvation, in as simple language as possible, stopping every few words to have it interpreted. Horace, who is a member of our mission church, followed with a few remarks, and we closed with prayer. The people listened with attention, saying that no one else had ever preached there. Our audience comprised a dozen adults and several children, yet these were nearly all the inhabitants.

Leaving this small village, we walked along a shady path to Bonthe, a large town, many of whose people speak English. The meetings are held in a barre, near the center of the place. A good-sized audience assembled, to whom we spoke from the words, "And ye will not come unto me that ye might have life." Opposite the barre is the kitchen of the town, and during the services I noticed several country women engaged in their work. A short recess followed the preaching, and then a Sabbath school was held. , It was nearly night when the school closed, and the tide was up so that we could not walk home. The chief, however, kindly sent us in a log canoe.

Dec. 25. — Last Sabbath I gathered about thirty people in Bro. Jewett's school-room. I took James for an interpreter. Hardly one of my audience attends the chapel services, as they do not understand English. I hoped to get a dozen together, and was agreeably disappointed to see so many. Mr. Jewett and James went about to their houses, and sent them in one by one. Some, as they came to the door, would stop and hesitate, as though afraid to enter; but as I pointed them to a seat, they would come in half bent, with a gliding, frightened motion. As I stood up to address that little, strange-looking company of heathen in the mud-walled school-house, I felt very deeply my need of strength from above. Our services were much as usual. More than ever do I perceive that it is not by might, nor by power, but by the Holy Spirit, that souls are led to Jesus.

A week ago I preached at Bendoo, a thriving village some five miles away. A boat was sent for me in the morning, and after an hour's ride, getting aground several times on the sand-banks, we reached the landing. I was warmly welcomed by several of the people at the beach. An audience of a hundred and twenty-nine assembled in the chapel, which is commodious, with rude seats, mud walls, thatched roof, and sand floor. Through the open windows came the breath of the tropics, and the noon-day sunshine rested on the luxuriant vegetation of this land of fruits and flowers. Everything was hushed and quiet, and as I looked on the neatly-dressed congregation before me, my heart overflowed with thanksgiving that I had been permitted to witness such a sight on Africa's shores.

Jan. 23.— Last Sabbath was a beautiful day, with a fine breeze. About nine I started for Keilah, distant some four miles. It was very pleasant sailing over the sparkling river that quiet morning, and I thanked God that I was thus permitted to go from place to place, bearing the glad tidings of salvation to those who sit in darkness. I was welcomed by the chief, who soon called his people together. I stood in the piazza of his country house, but most of the congregation were sitting on the ground under a large mango tree. They gazed earnestly into my face as I spoke awhile of Christ and their need of salvation. I promised to meet them again in two weeks, and, bidding them good-by, returned to Good Hope. After a half hour's rest and a lunch, I started for Bonthe. A goodly number were gathered in the barre. I had preached in the same place the Sabbath before, and now one man came to me wishing to be married to the woman with whom he had lived for some time, saying that he had been thinking about death, and he wanted to break off his sins. It was cheering to see that the truth had made some impression upon him. It was near night when I returned home, much wearied, but happy. These little gatherings in heathen towns and villages are very pleasant to the missionary. I shall not soon forget the Sabbaths spent under the mango tree or in the barre.

Feb. 1. — Leaving Keilah, we crossed over to Dumbuco, a village that was plundered a year ago by a war-party from the interior. It is dif-

ficult to get there at low tide, a wide strip of
swamp intervening between the river-side and
the town. A narrow, winding channel has been
dug through it, which is filled with water when
the tide is up. We passed up this channel, the
boat sometimes touching one side and sometimes the other. A few men stood watching us
as we landed. I inquired for the chief, but he
was not at home. A young man, however, conducted me to the house of the chief's mother,
an old woman, who was lying sick in a small
country house. She spoke broken English, and
seemed pleased when I told her that I had come
to talk about God. She called the people into
her little house, and Horace interpreted for me
as I tried to tell that group of heathen the story
of the cross. The country house where we held
the meeting was very rude and small. My com-
panion and I sat on a rough box. Some of the
heathen women seemed afraid to enter, but they
finally ventured to come and crouch on the hard
mud floor, and lean against the clay-plastered
wall. It was a strange but interesting scene as
I stood up to preach in that rude hut, with the

interpreter at my side. As we commenced the meeting there was some talking and noise, but the people soon became silent, and listened attentively. The chief's mother thanked us repeatedly for coming. We left with those feelings that the missionary among the heathen knows so well from experience when he has been trying in weakness and imperfection to sow the gospel seed.

Aug. 8.—Yesterday was the holy Sabbath. It dawned

"With breath all incense,
And with cheek all bloom."

After the long weeks of constant, heavy rains, it seemed very delightful to see such a beautiful morning. The sky was a soft, deep blue; the sunshine rested on the shining leaves of the trees; the river lay bright and still, just rippled by the light, cooling breeze; and the sweet song of birds came in through the open windows. The ride to York Island in the little blue boat, my "Sabbath home," was delightful; and all the way my soul welled up in a hymn of praise to God for the beauties that were visible. On-

ward we sped, now dashing across a wide strip
of blue, sparkling water, now creeping close
along the shore of a mangrove island, to avoid
the furious tide; now gliding over hushed waters, and now gently rocked by shining wavelets;
overhead the most entrancing of tropical skies,
dotted with floating clouds of fleecy white; the
distant horizon tinted with violet and azure;
on, meeting now and then a log canoe, with its
half-naked paddlers; on, past the queer little
town of Yellebanah, sleeping in the rich sunlight; round " the point," and then, borne
by the swift tide, quickly we reach the land-
ing-place. The brown mud houses, with their
thatched roofs, clustered beneath the giant cotton-trees and groves of cocoa, look very prettily.
The little bell was already ringing as I stepped
upon the beach, and soon a goodly congregation
had gathered in the spacious, airy country house
where our meetings are held. I spoke from the
first and second verses of the one hundred and
thirty-ninth Psalm. The groups seated around
me listened with attention. I was cheered by
the cordial welcome which I received, after be-

ing detained from them for two weeks by sickness.

From York Island to Bonthe I had another refreshing hour on the water. As we rounded the last mangrove island and came in sight of the long shore, the scene was striking. The horizon was clear, and here and there rose stately palms and giant cotton-trees. Seven villages were in sight; and as we passed along, now and then a boat or canoe could be seen gliding over the shining river. Far to the south-east, vailed with the lightest of haze, lay the shore of the continent. My audience was attentive, but not large, and the Sabbath school was deeply interesting.

In the beautiful moonlight eve we had a solemn meeting in the chapel. Oh that God's Spirit might be abundantly poured out upon us!

Oct. 18.—The absence of our small boat prevented my usual Sabbath preaching tour, but the day was not without its labors. Immediately after breakfast I went with my interpreter to a heathen village near by, hoping to be able to tell of Jesus to some who do not understand English. We found a group of people in one of the yards, seated together in a favorable position. Among them were several strangers from Gallinas, who had never before heard the word. I told them it was God's day, and we had come to talk to them about him. They thanked me, and said they would listen. One intelligent-looking woman, who seemed to be a sort of leader, did most of the talking. She wore an abundance of gree-grees on her neck and wrists. I related in simple words the story of God's love for us, and my young man interpreted. As I ended I invited them to ask any questions about the subject which they might wish. The head woman said that they had heard my word; it was true; they thanked me for it; they would remember it when they went home, and would try to obey God's teachings, and pray to him. I asked her why she wore gree-grees.

"They keep my life in me," she answered. I told her of the folly of such a trust, and that they did not help her at all. I asked her if she supposed that if she were drowning in the river the gree-grees could save her.

" Yes," she quickly replied.

" But I am alive," said I, " and do not wear gree-grees ; and so are many other people."

" But you are different from us ; if I was in America I would take them off, but here I do not dare to," she answered. " A murray-man gave them to me, and I have worn them ever since I was a little girl."

I told her that God was angry with us if we trusted in anything but him.

" You are different from us," she said ; " you are white and we are black."

" But God says that he has made of one blood all nations that dwell on the earth, and he will punish black and white alike for their sins."

She made no reply, and I continued : " You say that you believe there is but one God ; that is true ; so there can be but one way to serve him, and go where he dwells ; and if we trust in gree-grees, we do not walk in that way."

We continued our conversation for some

time through the interpreter. She clung to
her gree-grees, though she could give no reason
why they should help her. She gave evidence
of possessing a good mind, but it was crushed
and blighted by heathenism and its superstitions. As I left, she said, "I thank you for
what you have told me ; may God grant us both.
long life." Oh that the seed sown in her heart
on that Sabbath morning may bear fruit to eternal life !

Returning from Gondamar, I attended the
morning services at the chapel. At half-past
three came the Sabbath school. The attendance was good, and the hour passed pleasantly,
closing by singing, "I have a Father in the
promised land." The evening was clear and
calm, with a full moon. I preached to a large
audience from the words, "Jesus Christ, the
same yesterday, and to-day, and for ever."

CHAPTER XII.

A MISSIONARY TOUR.

APRIL 25.—Having a favorable opportunity, and feeling the need of a change, I left home on Tuesday morning for a short trip towards the interior of the country. The little blue boat, my Sabbath home, was rigged and manned, and we started about half-past ten. The day was one of the brightest and most beautiful that the tropics afford, and the ride for the first few hours was delightful; but while crossing the bar at the mouth of the Bargroo, the water became frightfully rough. A strong wind blew from the sea, and the waves rolled like ocean-billows. It seemed as though our little boat would be overwhelmed, but it rode gracefully over the towering waves, though the spray and billows broke over its side till we became thoroughly drenched. Soon the water became smoother, and following the windings of the Bargroo and the crooked Mahno, we reached Avery station about five P. M. Bro. Jewett gave me a cordial welcome, and we spent a pleasant evening in social converse and prayer.

Bro. Jewett kindly offered to accompany me on my journey to King Sissiwuru's town; and having made the needful arrangements, we left early on Wednesday morning. One of the king's sons was at Mahno, and we secured him as a guide. We returned to the mouth of the Mahno, and then entered the comparatively unknown Bargroo. The weather was bright and beautiful, the air soft and warm. We had a double object in the trip,—to tell the story of redeeming love in town and village, and to see and explore new regions.

We soon reached Yoggeh, a pleasant little town, situated in a palm-grove, on the left bank of the Bargroo. We landed at a large timber-factory near by, and walked to the old town of Yoggeh, passing several " country-fashion houses," built over portions of bug-a-bug hills. The land is elevated, the air fresh, the water cool, and many villages are seen a little back from the river. The groves of graceful palms diversified the appearance of the country.

Before ten we reached Kerrehhoo, a fine-looking town on a bluff, with a back-ground of tropical foliage ; but we had no time to call. Beyond Kerrehhoo the Bargroo grows narrower, and both banks are lined with large, tall mangroves, and hills and forests a little way back. The bright sunlight, a fresh breeze, and an easy, swift boat, made the voyage delightful.

Just beyond Kerrehhoo, we passed Mahno Mountain, a high elevation, partly covered with trees. This mountain is regarded as a kind of sacred place by the people, the residence of the great spirit Kasilon, before spoken of. At noon we passed Tassaw, a large town on the left bank of the stream. The people came in throngs to the river-side, to watch us as we passed. The country in the vicinity is hilly and rocky, and the river winding. Some two miles above Tassaw we left the Bargroo, and entered Mosandy

Creek, a small river whose general course is from the north-east. A short distance from the river-side there are beautiful groves of palm, and hills covered with forests. A half-hour further brought us to the town of Mosandy, situated on a slight elevation amid clusters of palms. Here, too, the people came flocking to the river-bank, but we could not stop. I noticed several little " country-fashion houses" perched on a high bank under the trees.

About 2 P. M. we arrived at Gondamar, beyond which we could not pass in our boat, on account of rocks. Taking a present in my hand, I called on Boondookeh, the king, and asked permission to leave the boat in his care. He consented, and all the portable articles were brought up, and shown to him, separately, so that nothing might be lost; they were then carefully packed away in his house. We knew that he would regard his promise as sacred, and that our things would be as safe as if defended by an armed guard. Without resting, we started forward on foot, intending to stop at the first town and cook our food. Our path lay through an open field, dotted with palms, while hills could be seen rising in the distance. A short walk brought us to Mo Bak, a new town, belonging to Sissiwuru. While the men were cooking, Bar Bak, the king, called some of his people together, and we preached to them through an interpreter. They spread their mats on the ground at our feet, and sat down, gazing earnestly at us, as we told them of God and the Saviour, occasionally clapping their hands, or making some exclamation of approval. After talking a while, we invited them to ask us any questions that they might wish to on the subject. In the course of my remarks, I had tried to show them the importance of praying to the great God who made us, instead of offering sacrifice to spirits, worshiping bug-a-bug hills and gree-grees; and now they eagerly inquired, "How can we pray so that God can hear us?" I tried to explain, and they seemed to comprehend. Bro. Jewett talked to them for some time with great plainness and earnestness, to which they listened with deep attention. We then joined in a short, simple prayer, which was interpreted into Sherbro. At the close, I told them that I hoped they would not forget the words we had spoken to them when we were far away, and never shall I forget the remarkable answer I received. It came from a heathen woman, ignorant of a word of English, who probably had never before heard of the Saviour from the lips of any one. She said, " Suppose you take a cassada-stick, cut it in two, and plant the pieces in the ground; soon it will sprout and grow.* So it will be with the word you drop in our hearts to-day; it can not die, but when you are far away it will spring up and grow." Oh, how that answer, coming from such a source, thrilled my soul, and rebuked my lack of faith! It was perfectly in accordance with the teachings of God's word, and no divine could have expressed it more forcibly.

We left Mo Bak about four o'clock in the afternoon. The nearest town on our route was

---

* Referring to the mode of propagating the cassada in Africa. When planted it seems a dry stick, but it soon grows to a large, flourishing bush.

more than twenty miles distant, and our path lay through a dense forest, infested with tigers, leopards, and elephants; but I felt that my time was so limited that I could not afford to delay until morning. Our party consisted of eight,—the son of King Sissiwuru for a guide, Bro. Jewett and myself, and five men to carry our light luggage. We started forward at a swift pace, and soon plunged into a thick, heavy forest. The road was a mere narrow foot-path, very crooked and rough, and we were often compelled to creep through the dense bush around some fallen tree, or crawl over the trunk for twenty or thirty feet. At first our company was somewhat scattered, and the path was so winding that we frequently lost sight of each other. The men in advance occasionally gave a shrill cry, which was answered by those in the rear; and now and then, as I strode swiftly onward, I caught sight of some one flying past a corner just before me. Towards sunset we reached a clear mountain stream, dashing over the rocks, and stopped a moment to quench our thirst with the cool, sparkling water. Again we pressed rapidly on, wishing to get as far as possible before darkness should set in. The country was hilly and rocky, the forest trees large and lofty, with a thick growth of underbrush. Night soon overtook us in the midst of the forest, many miles from the nearest town. The sky was beautifully clear, and the moon nearly full, but the spreading branches of the forest trees formed such an impenetrable arch that only now and then did a single ray of the soft moonlight pierce through, and rest like silver on the green shrubs by our path. We were compelled to moderate our pace a little, and walk as close to each other as possible, the guide carefully leading the way. Sometimes the path conducted us through a valley shrouded in almost total darkness, and we had to exercise the utmost caution to prevent falling over loose roots and stones. We knew that wild beasts roamed through the forest seeking for prey, but our faculties, both of body and mind, were so taxed in making our way through the bush, that we had no time to fear, or scarcely to think of them. Our guide was faithful, and, heathen man though he was, quite won my heart by his kindness. At every rough spot or difficult place he would stop, hold out his hand, and lead me gently over it. Often, during that night walk, I thought of the cheering answer of the poor heathen woman at Mo Bak, and my heart was encouraged.

Hour after hour we pressed forward in silence, and towards midnight reached a little clearing, in which stood the town of Mo Cassy. The people were still up, and crowded round us as we entered. I carried a present to the king, and told him we wished to rest in his town that night, and he at once provided us with a house. As we were reclining on mats in the rude piazza, I noticed that the people still lingered about in groups, conversing in their language, or watching us; so I sent word to the king that if he would call them together we would talk " God-word." They soon gathered to the number of seventy or eighty, and spreading their mats on the white sand in front of our mud-walled hut, they sat down to listen. The scene was strange and interesting. The hour was midnight; the

22

place, a rude town in the midst of an African forest; the hearers, a group of heathen sitting on mats at our feet; and over all rested the rich, soft light of a tropical moon. Though weary with our long night's walk, we rejoiced at the opportunity of repeating in their ears the story of redeeming love. The interpreter was not very skillful, but the people seemed to understand most that we said, and asked several questions. Perhaps none present had ever before heard about God from the lips of a missionary.

We were objects of much curiosity to the people. They were specially pleased with my watch and the glass lantern. At first, if the lantern chanced to be moved towards them, they sprang suddenly back, but soon lost their fear. We slept soundly that night on mats spread on the mud floor, very grateful to our kind heavenly Father for the manifold mercies of that eventful day and evening.

Early the next morning we again started forward. Near the town we passed some graves, on which a tin cup and a few other small arti-

cles had been laid as sacrifices to the spirits of
the dead. The country grew more hilly and
rocky as we advanced, and occasionally we had
to climb a steep ascent, or cross a deep gorge
on a narrow tree-trunk. A rapid walk of an
hour and a half brought us to the large rice
farms of Sissiwuru. Some single fields consisted of thirty or forty acres. The trees and bush
had been cut and set on fire, but large blackened trunks and limbs were lying in every direction, so that our passage was rendered difficult. A little beyond these fields we came to
Wallah, the capital of King Sissiwuru's country.
We passed in through the double gates, and
were at once conducted to the royal house,
where the king, surrounded by his chief counselors, was sitting in state to receive us. We
were shown into the house that had been prepared for us, a messenger having been dispatched
in advance to inform the king of our coming.
Mats were spread on the smooth clay floor,
and a dish of rice and fish set before us. We
did it full justice, and after having shaken hands
with a large number of people, a couch of mats

and country cloths was prepared, and we were invited to lie down and rest. The royal house which Sissiwuru set apart for me (probably because, being white, I was a greater curiosity than Bro. Jewett), was really a neat building. Like all African houses, it was constructed of clayey mud, but the walls were hard, smooth, and almost white. They were adorned on the outside with various rudely sketched figures, and on the inside hung with handsome mats and leopard-skins. The floor was smooth and solid. Bro. Jewett's house, a little way off, was also well furnished.

After resting myself, the window and door meanwhile thronged with a curious group watching my every motion, I selected a few presents and carried them to the king. Sissiwuru is a tall, dignified man, with a massive frame and majestic appearance. He was dressed in a flowing robe, somewhat ornamented, reaching a little below his knees; his feet were bare; a white sash was tied around his head, and in his hand he held a sort of scepter. He is the richest and most powerful king in the whole region, and has four or five walled towns, beside large numbers of villages. Sissiwuru has been a noted warrior, and has achieved many victories over neighboring tribes; but now he expressed a desire to live in peace with all. He is quite aged, but seems to have lost none of his native vigor and energy.

In company with his son, I passed around the town, and outside the gates. Wallah is very strongly fortified for an African town. The houses are necessarily very near each other, the thatched roofs often touching; and as there are no streets, a stranger will be quite likely to lose his way. Most of the houses are neat and substantial, and look really pretty, with their smooth, brown walls and covering of thatch. Many kitchens and barres, opening on one and sometimes all four sides, are scattered through the town, and in them the people often gather for conversation. The king's barre is the most beautiful country building that I have seen in Africa. It is circular in form, and the smooth thatched roof runs to a point, which is surmounted by a small cupola, and a figure of a

bird carved in wood. Two or three steps lead
up to the smooth floor. Four wooden pillars
support the roof. A smooth wall rises round
the elevated floor to the hight of some two feet,
and, though composed of a kind of mud, it ap-
pears as hard and smooth as freestone. Two
miniature cannon, perfectly formed from the
same substance, are placed on the wall at the
two entrances; and on one side is a sort of
carved chair, also of mud. A large hammock
is suspended in one part of the barre, in which
the king spends much of his time, surrounded
by fifteen or twenty of his chief men, who lie
on leopard-skins, or sit on the low, polished wall.
Most of them are armed with long, keen swords
of native manufacture.

I spent some time in this barre during the
day conversing with the king; and the novelty
of a white face always drew a crowd together.
A laugh was often raised by the sudden screams
of terror from the smaller children whenever I
chanced to approach them. Doubtless, many
of the people had never before seen a white
man. If we walked through the town, a group

of twenty or thirty were sure to follow, watching every motion ; and whichever way I turned I was certain to meet staring eyes.

Outside the walls of the town, the forest is cleared for some distance, so that no enemy can creep up unseen. Large numbers of African sheep, and a few cows, feed here during the day, but are driven within the walls at night. The Mahno river passes near Wallah, but during the dry season it is a mere brooklet. Its bed is filled with immense rocks. The country in the vicinity is hilly and stony, and the trees very large and lofty. The soil is rich, producing luxuriant crops with but little labor. The air is pure, the water clear, and the region altogether a delightful one. A chain of mountains, covered with heavy forests, lies to the northwest of Wallah. They are called by the natives the Koler Mountains, and are infested with tigers. Elephants are abundant in those forests, and are often killed. Some of Sissiwuru's people were on an elephant-hunt while we were there. Several large walled towns, and many villages, are situated within a few hours' walk of Wallah; but our time was too limited to permit us to visit them.

After a pleasant day in the place, we asked permission to preach, and the king promised to call the people together in the evening, when they came in from their farms. At twilight the town began to be thronged. Kitchen and barre were filled with talkative groups, passing to and fro. An hour after dark a messenger went around calling to the people to assemble in the name of the king. Bro. Jewett and myself had been sitting together, conversing and reading, and as we stepped out into the open space between the royal barre and the king's house, a sight met my eyes which I shall never forget. Barre, piazza, and country house were full, and tier upon tier of people were sitting on the white sand at our feet, forming a complete circle. Every eye was bent upon me. Overhead, in the tropical sky, rode the full moon, shedding its soft light on the scene, and a few stars looked faintly down. Standing in the midst of this interesting congregation, I told them in simple words about God and Christ.

An interpreter stood at my side, and rendered what I said into Sherbro. Another, with a commanding figure and a powerful voice, that could be heard far away, took the words from him and turned them into Mendi, so that all might understand. The people listened attentively, now and then making some sign of approbation. Bro. Jewett followed with some excellent remarks, and some questions were asked by the people. We closed with a short prayer, which also went through two interpreters. In the course of the prayer I remembered the king particularly, and at the close of every petition relating to him the people on all sides clapped their hands enthusiastically. This showed us that they loved their king, and understood, too, what we were saying. After the prayer, they soon scattered through the town, discussing among themselves what they had just heard. From a partial count, we judged that more than three hundred were present.

Early the next morning, we made preparations to return. Sissiwuru sent us a present of a sheep and fowls, and expressed much anx·

iety to have a school established in his town.
Our procession, as it issued from the gates of
Wallah and wound along the narrow path, numbered some thirty. Several of the king's sons
and war-men, armed with swords, accompanied
us as an escort. About a mile from the place,
most of them bade us good-by and returned,
though a few continued with us through the
day. We pressed rapidly on over the rough,
winding path, reaching Mo Cassy about ten,
A. M. We merely paused to get a drink of water, and bid Karfungbu, the king, good-by, and
then continued our journey. Hardly a ray of
the noonday sun pierced through the overhang-
ing branches of the trees, but still the air was
very hot. Hour after hour passed, and we continued our rapid pace, till I felt like sinking to
the earth with fatigue.

Towards night we reached Gondamar, where
we had left our boat, having walked thirty miles
over a rough path without stopping. We were
just in season to obtain shelter from a heavy
tornado. While the men were cooking, we
threw ourselves on some mats in the king's

house to rest. Every article that we had left in Boondookeh's care was safe. The tornado was soon over, and the setting sun came out in all its glory behind a grove of palms. The king summoned his people, and while the men were rigging the boat we preached in the barre to an attentive audience of eighty. They said that they believed the word we spoke, was true, and they would try to pray to God, and had some questions to ask about him. They seemed to receive the gospel with gladness; oh that those few words might be blessed to their salvation! A few feet from where I stood was a sort of altar, on which sacrifices are offered to spirits.

Bidding Boondookeh good-by, we hastened to the boat, nearly the whole town following us. Soon we were gliding swiftly down Mosandy Creek in the beautiful moonlight. After the weary walk of the day, we were well prepared to enjoy the quiet scene. It was really lovely when we entered the Bargroo. Above us stretched the clear, blue heavens; far to the south glowed the mild Southern Cross, and low in the northern sky we could just distinguish

the north star.   The ascending moon flooded
the river with silvery light, save where the bordering mangroves cast a dark, weird shade.
Now and then we passed a picturesque town on
the river bank.   It was almost midnight when
we reached Avery.   The next day I returned to
Good Hope, feeling that truly God had fulfilled
to me those sweet promises recorded in the
ninety-first Psalm.

CHAPTER XIII.

THE English colony of Sierra Leone is some-times called " the stronghold of missions " on the coast of West Africa. And per-haps it deserves that name, for it is indeed a bright spot, from whence good influences are being diffused among the surrounding tribes. In many respects it is far inferior to Liberia, yet as a missionary center it may be regarded as fully its equal.

The colony was established about a century ago, and occupies a peninsula containing some three hundred square miles. This peninsula is situated in latitude 8° 30′ N., and is bounded on one side by the Sierra Leone River, and on the other by the Atlantic Ocean. Its scenery is said to be finer than that of any other point on

181

the western coast of Africa. No traveler, approaching its harbor after a weary sea-voyage, can remain an indifferent spectator of the scene that rises before his eyes. At first the mountains loom up faint and blue, lying cloud-like in the far horizon; but, as he nears the coast, each peak gradually assumes its own peculiar shape, and, crowned with a wealth of foliage, towers against a back-ground of dreamy tropical sky. A few green open slopes and cultivated patches, with here and there a pretty village perched on the hill-side, vary the prospect; while on a narrow plain, between the foot of the mountain and the Sierra Leone River, lies Freetown, the chief city, and capital of the colony. A few vessels are anchored in the harbor, and opposite the town, across the bay-like mouth of the river, the eye discovers the low, level Bullom shore, stretching away in the distance. Over all rests that soft haze which is peculiar to the tropics, hiding every harsh outline and uncouth feature, and causing the whole view to seem almost like the scenery of a fairy tale. The graceful palms, that stand like sentinels along the beach, their long plumes bending idly in the air; the beautiful cocoa-nut, with its clusters of fruit surrounding the parent stem; the luxuriant orchards of banana and plantain, loaded with huge bunches of ripening fruit, and the long, broad leaves shining in the sunlight; the pyramidal bread-fruit, the fragrant orange, the blossoming lime-hedge, with numerous other foreign-looking trees, shrubs, and flowering vines, all conspire to rivet the gaze of the looker-on, and fill him with admiration.

In a commercial point of view, Sierra Leone is a place of some importance. Vessels from all parts of the world frequent its harbor, bringing the merchandise of other countries in exchange for palm-oil, hides, ground-nuts, &c., which are procured up the rivers, and brought down by native traders in rude canoes. Several foreign traders have established themselves in the colony, and are doing a thriving business in this trade; but a large part of the business of Sierra Leone is transacted through the native merchants. Some of these exhibit a good deal of sagacity, and have acquired considerable wealth. Many of them have had to struggle with great difficulties, and by their perseverance have overcome obstacles at which even some New England boys would have been daunted. The history of many a Sierra Leone man effectually shows that the African is possessed of more native ability than many have been wont to believe. One of the leading merchants whom I met there was stolen when a child from the far interior. Fortunately, the vessel in which he was confined was captured by the English fleet, and he was liberated at Freetown. But he was a poor boy, alone among strangers, and surrounded by heathen influences. He struggled on amid many trials and disappointments, and now he owns a store in Freetown which would be no disgrace to an American city; and, what is better, he is an active Christian man. Other cases, as marked as this, might be narrated, and, if the history were fully given, it would certainly contain many touching incidents and strange, wild adventures, as well as forcibly illustrate the power of well-directed effort even in heathen Africa.

The population of Sierra Leone is variously estimated. Its chief city, Freetown, is supposed to contain thirty thousand inhabitants; and perhaps there are as many more in the towns and villages scattered among the romantic hills and valleys of the colony. The population may be divided into three classes,—foreign residents, educated natives, and common people. There are also many subdivisions of the people depending on the tribe or country from which they originally came. The foreign residents are few in number, and comprise missionaries, government officers, and traders. The missionaries are chiefly supported by the Established Church, and Wesleyan Methodist, Societies of England, and, notwithstanding the idle tales of want of success, told by some travelers who have spent three or four days in the colony, and gone away laden with that superabundant wisdom which such temporary sojourns always beget, they are doing a most excellent work. It must be confessed, however, that the influence of many of the traders and government officials is anything but favorable to the morals of the people. The

24

second class, educated natives, comprise minis-
ters, lawyers, physicians, editors, teachers, merchants, mechanics, and others who have enjoyed
the advantages of schools. The attainments of
some are very limited, but a few would rank
quite high as scholars. The educated class is
increasing year by year, and it is hoped that
they will soon outnumber the lower class, who
now form the larger part of the population.
Many of the latter profess Christianity, but they
mingle with their worship and belief many relics of heathenism. Others still cling to their
olden ways.

A few of the early settlers of Sierra Leone
came from Nova Scotia,—free negroes, who had
aided the British during the American Revolu-
tionary war, and for whom they felt bound to
provide ; but nearly all of the present inhabitants are " liberated Africans " and their de-
scendants. The term " liberated Africans " is
applied to such as have been rescued from slave-
barracoons and slave-ships on the African coast.
Sierra Leone, consequently, is almost entirely
peopled by those who have been rescued from

the fearful doom of slavery, and have found here a refuge and a home.

Freetown, the capital and chief town of the colony, is a city of strange extremes. Civilization and barbarism meet in its streets and walk side by side. The contrasts are striking, and sometimes ludicrous. Here goes an English lady, with rustling silks and spotless muslin; and closely following is a poor heathen woman, half naked, with chalk-marked face and grotesquely-braided hair. Yonder is a Frenchman, attired in the latest Parisian styles; and a few steps behind him a stately Mohammedan from the interior, his flowing robe reaching from his shoulders nearly to the ground, and his arms and neck hung with an abundance of gree-grees. Market-women go chatting along the streets, balancing their "blies" of fruit and vegetables on their heads; and little children, destitute of any covering, toddle after them. There is no roar of carriages, but the ever-passing throngs keep up a constant stream of talk, varied with frequent shrill exclamations and bursts of laughter. This noise sometimes becomes almost deafening, especially in the narrow streets, which are lined with shops, where excited crowds gather round the different stands, eagerly intent on driving a bargain. Many of the people, in their intercourse with each other, use the language of the tribe to which they belong ; and as there are representatives of sixty or seventy tribes in Freetown, as many different languages are spoken. Nearly all, however, speak a broken English, which furnishes a universal medium of communication.

The foreign residents and better class of natives live in frame or stone houses, often furnished luxuriantly with carpets, sofas, and other articles of furniture imported from Europe. The larger portion of the houses, however, are built in native style, and of course are very rude.

Some extracts from my journal during a brief residence in Sierra Leone, though they may prove somewhat egotistic, will, perhaps, give a better picture of life there than any general remarks that I can make. The first extract will relate more particularly to a journey

SIERRA LEONE. 189

from our mission to Freetown, a distance of about a hundred miles.

Freetown, Aug. 29.—We were obliged to leave Good Hope for a short sojourn among the hills, on account of Mrs. Whiton's failing health. The morning was cloudy and wet, and as we bade good-by to the group gathered on the wharf, a strange feeling of sadness crept over us. We had ten oarsmen, a captain, and one of the mission girls. Our little "Olive Branch" was quite comfortable, with its rain-awning and mattress-cushioned seats, pillows, shawls, &c. Mrs. W. lay weak and sick on one side, and I sat on the other, while trunks and boxes formed a barricade in front. At "the Point" we anchored for half an hour for the men to eat breakfast, and then, as a breeze sprung up, we glided along the island shore, passing now and then a village reposing among palms and tropical trees. About two P. M. we passed Jenkins, where in 1816 Samuel J. Mills came to select a spot for the colonization of free colored people from the United States. The first ship-load was landed there, many of whom died in a few

. weeks from the fever, brought on by exposure and lack of comforts. Several missionaries who accompanied them also sleep their last sleep near the white sand beach at Jenkins. Mournful thoughts filled my mind as we were passing, and I felt thankful to God that he had raised up men who were willing to toil, suffer, and die as pioneers in the great work of missions on this deadly coast.

Soon after passing Jenkins a strong head wind set in, and as the tide was against us we were obliged to anchor. The rain fell in torrents, and the boat rocked so much that we all became sea-sick. As darkness shut down, the prospect seemed discouraging, for, though at this season we always look for southerly winds, the breeze continued to blow strongly from the north. The rain found its way through the awning, and pattered down upon our blankets and mattresses. At ten in the night, when the tide turned, I roused the men, who were sleeping around a fire in the bow of the boat with a sail spread over them, and directed them to take the oars. They were reluctant to leave their snuggery, but by means of persuasion and command I managed to get ten oars at work. If I chanced to sleep for an hour, the men were almost sure to stop pulling; but by frequent shouts and persuasions we were able to get forward at tolerable speed. Morning found us in sight of Shingy, with no wind and a contrary tide. About ten we landed at the wharf. The water was quite rough, and as the men took us in their arms to carry us ashore they were obliged to run up the beach to prevent our being drenched by the next wave. We walked to the mission-house, now empty, and rested in the cool, airy sitting-room. Shingy is beautifully situated on a high point, and enjoys a fine sea breeze. The native town is some distance off, but quite large. In front you gaze over the boundless ocean, and in a clear day can see the Banana Islands and the mountains of Sierra Leone.

About noon we started across Yawry Bay with a splendid breeze from the north-west. We found the water quite rough, but the "Olive Branch" bounded from wave to wave,

flinging the spray from her bow, and in three
hours we were at Kent.   The view in crossing
the bay was delightful.   The sun shone brightly
on the heaving waters; the low, level coast
back of the bay was visible now and then; the
lofty mountains of Sierra Leone rose grandly
in front; and the Banana Islands lay like green
gems in the shining sea.   As we glided swiftly
along under full sail, we had a fine view of
Kent, lying in quiet beauty on the hill-side.   In
passing the reef we came near going ashore
through the carelessness of our captain.   The
huge breakers tossed our boat like a dry leaf,
but soon we rounded the point, and glided up
to the beach between two rocky ledges.

Next morning we continued our voyage.
With a light breeze we crept along the coast,
passing one after another the green mountains
and peaceful villages.   York is the largest town
in the vicinity, and lies on the side of a high
hill, presenting a beautiful appearance as the
traveler passes in a boat.   The summits of
some of the mountains were vailed in clouds,
and occasionally a light shower passed along

their sides. The wind at length veered to the north, and our progress was slow. Just before dark we passed False Cape. The tide was low, and the heavy ocean swells dashed in foaming fury against the huge black rocks that line the cape. As we were passing, the setting sun came out in glory, tinging the water and distant hills with beauty. The night-shadows soon gathered around, and we rapidly neared Cape Sierra Leone. The light from the great lantern in the tower shone far out at sea, and faint glimmerings on the hills told us where the villages were situated. About ten o'clock we landed at King Jimmy's wharf in Freetown, and passing up a flight of stone steps, we found ourselves in the midst of more civilization than we had seen for many long months.

September 2.—Last Sunday morning dawned wet and rainy, but as the hour for service approached, the sun came out, and made walking more tolerable. I fulfilled a preaching engagement at a Wesleyan church in Rawdon Street. The chapel has a very humble exterior; low, stone walls, and a roof of bamboo thatch.

25

Within, it is plain, but spacious and comfortable. We found only a small audience assembled, but others came in during prayers. The congregation were very attentive. One old woman I particularly noticed; she sat in a corner, the tears rolling down her cheeks, while now and then a smothered sob escaped her. Others seemed much affected, and I trust the Holy Spirit was present. I was deeply interested with my morning experience in that humble thatched chapel.

In the eve I spoke again in the Lady Huntingdon Chapel. The rain was falling, but a goodly number gathered. This chapel is much more imposing in appearance than the Wesleyan. Galleries extend across three sides, and the body of the church is somewhat ornamented. It was brilliantly lighted, and the music was both instrumental and vocal.

On Saturday I enjoyed a pleasant walk to Fourah Bay, where a college for the education of native youths has been established by the English Church Missionary Society. I was cordially received by the President, and conducted over the building. The piazzas and halls are large and airy; the library cozy and American-like; and the students' rooms reminded me of my own early school-days. The grounds are pleasantly laid out, and a fine sea breeze comes from the water. In the distance rise lofty mountains, dotted here and there with cultivated farms and villages; the beautiful city of Freetown is in full view, while far away stretches the boundless ocean; and on the opposite side of the river lies the long, low Bullom shore. The road from Freetown to Fourah Bay is delightful. First we pass down Kissy Road, the Broadway of the place, which is lined with shops full of gay-colored goods, cloths, beads, earthen ware, and an endless variety of articles. Pedestrians, in every variety of dress that many-costumed Africa can show, throng the street, or stand at the shop-doors, driving bargains with the salesmen. It is a strange, curious sight for foreign eyes to gaze upon. Leaving Kissy Road, we pass over a stone bridge, under which dashes a mountain torrent, and then wind along a broad, smooth path, bordered with humble cottages.

Occasionally we catch a glimpse of the sea through the tree-branches, or of the farms on the hill-side. Much of the path is shaded by branching trees, which afford a cooling shade to the tired traveler.

Even barbarous Africa is not destitute of elegant residences, as a day at the country-house of one of the native merchants has abundantly convinced me. It is beautifully located on the sea-shore. On one side rise the mountains of the interior, and on the other you have a view of the opposite shore and far-stretching ocean. Freetown and the shipping in the harbor are partly seen through the wealth of tropical foliage. The house is commodious, and luxuriantly furnished. It stands on a bluff many feet above the river. Immense perpendicular walls of solid stone have been built to prevent the sea from encroaching upon the grounds, and a flight of eighty-one steps leads down to the water's side. As I wandered through the spacious saloons and elegant drawing-room, I could scarcely realize that I was in Africa. We spent a pleasant day, and in the evening attended a prayer-meeting.

Last eve, towards sunset, I took a little walk among the hills. Passing along Rawdon Street, I found myself in a part of the town that I had not before visited, and yet a most pleasant place. There was an abundance of shrubbery, and now and then a little rivulet dashing along over its stony bed. Narrow, shady lanes, lined with bamboo cottages, branched out in every direction. Soon I reached the foot of the mountains, and the path grew very steep. It was warm, toilsome work to ascend, but occasionally I paused to catch a breath of cooling air, and enjoy a glimpse of the scenery below, which every moment grew more surpassingly lovely. The path became steeper and steeper, but the cool mountain air was invigorating. At length I left the Regent road, and turned up a narrow path through a dense forest. The trees formed a green arch above, and the bed of the road was one mass of rock and loose stone. Sometimes the ascent was nearly perpendicular, and next I wound along the edge of a precipice. A half

hour of vigorous walking and scrambling
brought me to the top of one of the lower
mountains, on which stands the country-house
of a native merchant. The view from the sum-
mit was grand and beautiful, — such as no pen
can ever describe. Far, far below at my feet
lay the city and harbor, forming a picture of
strange loveliness. The houses seemed in miniature, and as the eye wandered over them it
could trace out the different streets and more
prominent buildings. The pedestrians below
looked like moving dolls. Far to the westward
lay the blue Atlantic, dotted here and there
with a snowy sail; and to the right, like a sea
of green, stretched the Bullom shore, vailed
with a soft haze. The tall palms at the cape
were plainly seen, and in the back-ground, one
above another, rose the forest-clad mountains,
till the eye rested on the vailed peak of " Sugar-
loaf." I stood entranced by the sight, as the
setting sun flooded the whole with a soft, rich
light; and then, gathering a handful of flowers,
I prepared to descend. This was soon accomplished, and as the evening shadows fell I

threaded the quiet streets homeward, not only refreshed by the ramble, but with my spirit inwardly rejoicing over a new leaf in the wondrous book of nature that had just been spread before me.

Saturday. — I enjoy very much the pleasant walks through the city and its suburbs. In Sherbro we have no roads, and the fine, smooth paths of Sierra Leone, though they would not be dignified by the name of roads in America, seem much like civilization. Yesterday afternoon I visited the cemetery back of Tower Hill, and spent an hour or two in rambling among the tombs. The sun was hot, but an umbrella tempered its rays, and an occasional rest under some tree was grateful. A few convicts from the chain-gang were clearing the paths, but most of the enclosure was overgrown with rank grass and bushes, — indeed, in the rains it is almost impossible to keep the grounds in tolerable order. There are many monuments scattered about, often with no inscription. The chief features of interest to me, however, were the graves of missionaries, who are buried here in large numbers. Some of the graves are un-marked, but the sleeping dust beneath is watched over by God, and at the resurrection of the just it shall arise clothed in immortality. Two members of our mission — the pioneer Raymond and Mr. Mair — rest there ; but no monument marks the spot, and I was unable to find it. Their record is in heaven. I noticed the graves of two English bishops, and of many Church, Wesleyan, and United Methodist missionaries. Two large white marble slabs mark the resting-place of two young Americans, — one from Boston and one from New York. In one part of the ground, under a large tree, are five monuments, side by side, where lie the bodies of five Roman Catholic missionaries, who came to the colony some years ago to establish their religion. They all fell victims to the climate a few weeks after landing. Many regarded their sudden removal as a special providence to prevent the establishment of a false religion.

Sept. 6. — As I was returning, the other day, from a visit at the Wesleyan mission-house, I paused for a few moments on a large stone

bridge, and gazed up the narrow gorge towards
the mountains. Far below dashed a pretty little stream, which is sometimes swollen to a
mountain torrent. Some women and children
were standing among the rocks, washing clothes.
Along the path on which I stood was a constant
procession of people,—many of them were returning to their homes in the villages from the
market, and nearly all carried large blies on
their heads. A portion of the town was in
sight, and in the distance rose the mountains,
their sides dotted with farms, presenting a most
pleasing landscape.

I walked slowly homeward, passing up Krootown Road, which, like Kissy, is lined with
shops full of gay cloths, trinkets, knives, scis-
sors, and almost everything imaginable. The
sun shone brightly, and all the streets were
thronged with pedestrians, presenting a busy
scene. Many of the women wore flowing dresses
of bright calico of different colors, and gay turbans on their heads; so that as you gazed down
a long street the view was really brilliant. The
passengers were laughing and chatting with

each other, or driving bargains with the shop-keepers.

Walking along the streets, I turned my steps toward the market. It was Saturday, the great market-day of the week, and the roar of voices as I approached was almost deafening. Outside the walls was spread a great variety of vegetables and fruits, which the owners were using every effort to dispose of. Passing up to the entrance, a most interesting sight met my eyes. The long building was crowded with people, and every stand seemed groaning beneath its load. There were heaps of fragrant oranges, and limes, and pine-apples; bunches of golden bananas, and long green plantains; cocoa-nuts, African pears, sour and sweet sop, sweet potatoes, cucumbers, yams, cocoa, eggs, green corn, water-cresses, string-beans, cabbages, turnips, greens, tomatoes, etc. Some tables were filled with beads of brilliant colors, knives, and various knick-knacks; some with small loaves of bread. At one end of the market lay heaps of " foofoo," which is made of beaten cassada, rolled in balls. This is considered a great del-

icacy by the natives, but would hardly tempt
the appetite of a foreigner. But I was not permitted to make my survey in quiet. The appearance of a white face is always the signal for
redoubled efforts on the part of the market-
women to dispose of their articles. "Master!"
"Master!" "Master!" came from every side,
and samples of fruit and vegetables were thrust
before me. If I had been a stranger I might
have lost my self-possession amid the confusion,
but I had so often been in the same position,
that I merely shook my head or uttered a quiet
"No" to their importunities, and examined
the tables at my leisure.

Freetown, Sept. 15.—Last week Wednesday
morning we left on our intended trip to the
mountains. At dawn it was quite rainy, but
the blue sky soon appeared, and gave token of
a favorable day. Our procession, as it left the
yard and wound mountain-ward, was thus: first,
Mrs. W. in a palanquin, with two faithful carriers; next myself, followed by our man John,
balancing a tin trunk on his head; and finally
Ellen, one of the mission-girls. Soon we left

the noisy streets and shady lanes of Freetown,
and began to climb the steep mountain-paths.
The scenery was very beautiful. One moment
the eye rested on cloud-capped peaks, rocky
gorges, roaring torrents, and steep precipices;
and the next on gently-sloping hill-sides and
lovely sun-lit valleys.

But it was not all romance, for climbing pre-
cipitous mountain-paths under a torrid sun is
by no means play. Behold me, toiling up the
rocks, an umbrella in one hand, and my hat,
which I use as a fan, in the other, exclaiming
one moment, "How beautiful!" and the next,
"Oh how hot!" As we ascended, the air grew
purer and cooler, and the sun was obscured by
clouds. Occasionally we sat down on some
rock to rest, and let imagination have full play
as we drank in the beauties of the scene.

By and by we descended to the romantic little village of Gloucester. Its thatched houses
are perched on steep hill-sides and in narrow
gorges, surrounded by cultivated patches. A
pretty stream goes dashing over the rocks. As
we crossed the stone bridge and wound up a

shady path, I might almost have imagined myself in a New England forest road, had it not been for the broad leaves of the banana and plantain, and the groves of palm and cocoa that everywhere met the eye.

Passing over another mountain, we came to Regent, a village containing some fifteen hundred inhabitants. It is built on both sides of a beautiful stream, and surrounded on every side by lofty mountains. The highest peak is Sugar-loaf, which is much of the time vailed in clouds. We were most cordially received by the native pastor, Rev. George Nicol, whose wife is a daughter of the celebrated Bishop Crowther, and a day in that romantic and beautiful village was full of interest.

On Thursday we visited Charlotte, four miles further. The scenery, if possible, was still grander than that of the previous day. The paths were quite slippery from recent rains, and it required considerable exertion to maintain one's footing. We passed the pretty village of Bathurst, following the course of a mountain stream, bordered with tropical foliage and gorgeous flowers. Two or three waterfalls were in sight among the hills. At Charlotte we found a large girls' school for liberated Africans. The pupils numbered upwards of a hundred, and are not only taught the common English branches, but are particularly instructed in industrial pursuits. Such a work requires much patience on the part of missionaries, but it is a blessed cause.

We left Charlotte Friday noon on our return to town by way of Wilberforce. It was a bright day, and most of the mountain-peaks were unvailed. The path lay over high table-lands, and the views of land and sea were enchanting. We rested at Wilberforce till nearly sundown. It is a pretty village on a mountain, in full view of Freetown and the harbor. Both the English Church and Wesleyans have mission stations here. We joined our good friend, Rev. Mr. Caiger, in a pic-nic dinner and pleasant ramble over the town. In the cool of the evening the palanquin-carriers trotted swiftly homeward. As we left the quiet outskirts of the city and entered Krootown Road, the noise seemed deafening. The street was thronged with pedestrians, talking, screaming, and laughing, and the carriers at almost every step were compelled to shout to them to clear the way. It was quite dark when we arrived, much pleased with our trip among the mountains.

Sierra Leone is certainly a wonderful example of what can be accomplished through God's blessing on missionary labor. There are nearly a hundred churches, and more than twenty thousand church-members, in the colony. Sabbath and day schools are everywhere established; also academies, female seminaries, and one college. Colored policemen patrol the streets; colored lawyers plead at the bar; colored pastors preach to colored audiences; and colored editors write for colored readers.

The Sabbath is better observed in Sierra Leone than in many American cities. The people are regular in their attendance at the house of God, and reverential in their deportment. Of course there is much wickedness, but still the changes there have been wonderful. Where once the cloud of heathenism brooded so heavily, the Sabbath bell now sends forth its glad sound. Where the human victim lay bleeding on the altar, now ascends the daily sacrifice of prayer and praise. And year by year this blessed light is spreading towards the tribes yet farther inland.

THE END.

www.ingramcontent.com/pod-product-compliance
Lightning Source LLC
Chambersburg PA
CBHW030823270326
41928CB00007B/869